The Energy Of Forgiveness

Finding Peace In A World Of Hurt

Paul McKinley

AM-PM Publishing

AM-PM Publishing
116 Charles St.
Gordonsville VA 22942

Cover created by:
Amy Barroso, White Lightening Communications
http://www.facebook.com/WhiteLighteningCommunications

Copyright © 2017 by Paul McKinley

First paperback printing December 2017

All rights reserved. This book may not be reproduced in whole or in part, stored in a retrieval system, or transmitted in any form or by any means electronic, mechanical, or other without written permission from the publisher, except by a reviewer, who may quote brief passages in a review.

ISBN 978-0-9971198-1-7

Contents

Chapter 1	Forgiveness Is Important	1
Chapter 2	The "Rules" Paradigm	9
Chapter 3	The Reality Inversion	23
Chapter 4	The Origins Of Forgiveness	37
Chapter 5	The Process Of Grieving	51
Chapter 6	What It Means To Forgive	61
Chapter 7	The Energy Of Forgiveness	69
Chapter 8	The Emotional Origins Of Dis-Ease	83
Chapter 9	The Penalty For Unforgiveness	91
Chapter 10	When Forgiving Seems Impossible	105

Refusing to forgive is like grabbing a red hot iron bar and shaking it at the unforgiven.

-- Paul McKinley

For Mike,

The end of your journey became the beginning of mine.

For Ann,

Who encourages me, who blesses me with her own insights, and acts as my sounding board for the ideas that became this book – and beyond.

For Eva Mozes Kor

You have taken the road less travelled. You are a blessing to mankind and to everyone who hears your message. The world is a better place because of you.

For my spiritual brothers and sisters in the Unity movement, especially Unity of Temple in Temple TX,

For helping me realize that mankind needed me to write "Rules Of The Spirit," which led to this book.

Testimonials

"I once called Paul my go-to-guy. As soon as the words left my mouth, I knew I really meant it. He is empathic. He gets you. He gets people. He really knows how to connect with others because he understands them at his core. If anyone says you can forgive and means it, it's Paul. He is gentle, caring spirit and a real heart. He wants nothing but healing for you. This book is his gift to you."

— Karyn Mullen
Philanthropist, Entrepreneur, former CEO

"Paul McKinley is a brilliant author who unlocks truths that are life transforming. "

—Jeff Ramsperger
award winning author of
the Big Shot book series

"Having come to know Paul and Ann socially and through working with them on a healing workshop I can say that they are two of the most sincerely caring and conscientious people I know, both applying their high intellect and genuine love for humanity to heal and bring peace to the world through their work. They have much to offer and I highly recommend their books and teachings, which will absolutely bring positive change into your life."

— Audrey Simpson-Campbell, BSc
Hypnotist and author of
"Metamorphosis: Pathway to
Personal Transformation"

"Paul's techniques and exercises on understanding The Energy of Forgiveness are insightful and incredibly healing. They have personally helped me find peace in my heart."

— Amy Barroso
author of "Why Can't We Be Friends"
and co-owner of The Creative Zoo
a shared office and services provider

"Paul McKinley is very nice guy and so positive about life and future. I had a great conversation with him about life and forgiveness. Although he is Christian, his words about forgiveness will help any person with any type of belief. I enjoyed his conversation and logic behind that and of course his book, Rules of the Spirit - Integrating Spiritual Truths In Daily Living. This book is awesome and so valuable and worth to be read more than once. His purpose of this book is helping people. I highly recommend his book. It brings peace and happiness to your life."
-Nooshin Adl

"As a frequent guest speaker at Unity of Temple, Paul's messages were always looked to with anticipation and joy. As he'd slow-walk the group through various concepts of being, in short order, the congregation would be silently nodding their heads in full agreement. From his messages came deeper perspectives on truth and how it relates to common everyday events. Albeit likely unnoticed by most at the time, Paul was dropping seed and supplying spiritual nourishment that, even today, produces meaningful impact in the lives of those who frequent the little Unity church in the heart of Central Texas."

— Russell Jones, US Army Ret.

"As a notable resource of knowledge for daily living, Paul takes one on a journey into Spirit by providing simple eye-opening concepts, enhancing understanding and facilitating the practical application of spiritual principles. Typical thinking expands as one is inspired to delve deeper and draw from Spirit, the strength and power to be true expressions of our greater selves."

-- Mary Parrish, Author of
Be Still and Know, Meditation for Beginners

Co-Author with Lisa Nichols of
*Living Proof: Celebrating the Gifts
That Came Wrapped in Sandpaper*

Acknowledgements

First of all, I'd like to give thanks to Raymond Aaron, whose 10-10-10 program provided both the framework and impetus that helped me get this book done as well as my first book *The Rules of the Spirit*. I had started writing bits and pieces of *The Rules of the Spirit* before I came across his program, but I would probably still just be thinking about it rather than getting it done. Now I have written two books! There are lots of mentors out there; Raymond is distinguished by his integrity. Go to http://10-10-10program.com/ and get started writing *your* book today!

Many thanks to Eva Mozes Kor who provided the foreword for this book. Your life experience, your ability to forgive, and your teaching about forgiveness is doing much to heal the world.

Many years ago, I was encouraged to speak by Rev. Jim Chandler, then senior pastor of Round Rock First United Methodist Church in Round Rock, Texas. Jim trusted me to speak the truth. That led to my becoming a Layspeaker, and things have evolved from that point.

My wife Ann has also provided encouragement and insights that help along the way. It's been a long process, but she's been there for me and provided the gentle accountability I needed along the way.

There have been too many friends to list from my spiritual community who encouraged me to write my first book *The Rules of the Spirit* with their questions of "When are you going to write a book about this?" This book is a natural sequel to *The Rules of the Spirit*. What I found is that in the process of writing *The Rules of the Spirit*, people were frequently showing up in my life that needed help with forgiveness – people who needed to hear exactly the message that I had to give. That is what led me to realize that there is such a great need for teachers in this world who can help people work through forgiveness – to release the negative energy and be able to thrive again in all areas of their lives.

Foreword

I am an Auschwitz survivor. I was taken to the camp in May 1944 along with my parents and three sisters. My parents and older sisters were murdered, I never saw them again. But my twin sister Miriam and I became subjects in Dr. Mengele's experiments, in the group of "Mengele twins." Both Miriam and I survived this experience, however Miriam died June 1993 from complications likely related to the Mengele experiments.

In August 1993 I had an opportunity to go talk with Dr. Munsch, who was an attending physician at the gas chambers in Auschwitz. He agreed to sign a document describing what he had seen at Auschwitz. I wanted to thank this doctor for agreeing to sign the document, and decided the best way was to write a letter of forgiveness for him.

What I discovered for myself through this act was life-changing. I discovered that I had the power to forgive. And that became an interesting thing, because as a victim of over 50 years I never felt that I had any power over my life. After that, and through the encouragement of my english professor, I also was able to forgive Dr. Mengele, the one who had presided over the horrible experiments on myself and other "Mengele twins." It made me feel very good, that I, the little guinea pig of 50 years even had the power over the "angel of death" of Auschwitz. After signing my Declaration of Amnesty with Dr. Munsch at Auschwitz, I felt free. Free from Auschwitz, free from Mengele.

But what is my forgiveness? I like it! It is an act of self-healing, self-libration, self-empowerment. All victims are hurt, feel hopeless, feel helpless, feel powerless.

I want everybody to remember that we *cannot change what happened*. That is the tragic part. But we *can* change how we relate to it!

I want the world to understand. My forgiveness has nothing to do with the perpetrator. It has nothing to do with any religion. I belive that I have the human right to live free of whatever was imposed on me. And I believe that every human being does!

Forgiveness is more than "letting go." It is proactive rather than passive. We become victims involuntarily, when a person or entity with power takes away our power to use our mind and body in the way we choose. Something was done to us that put us in a position of feeling powerless. Thus the conscious choice to forgive provides healing, liberation, and reclamation of this power.

Forgiving is not forgetting. It is in many cases impossible to forget events that deeply affect us. They shape our lives for better or worse. In the case of the Holocaust, it is important to remember and to teach the world what happened and to teach victims to heal through forgiveness because only forgiveness will heal the world and prevent another genocide.

Anger is a seed for war. Forgiveness is a seed for peace.

Eva Mozes Kor
  International authority on Forgiveness
  Founding Director of Candles Holocaust Museum and Education Center
  Author of
    "Surviving the Angel of Death"
    "Echoes of Auschwitz"
    "Little Eva and Miriam in the 1st Grade" and
    "The Power of Forgiveness" (German)

Chapter 1
Forgiveness Is Important

"There is little room left for wisdom when one is full of judgment."
— Malcolm Hein

Beginnings

I wrote my first book *The Rules of the Spirit* to collect into one place the major insights that I'd had over the years. The title of the book is based on what I call the "Rules" paradigm covered in Chapter 3 and elaborated in Chapters 4-6, which defines the basic rules that characterize Spirit, compared with the rules that characterize the World. Understanding this "Rules" paradigm helps you to recognize behaviors, in yourself or others, as being spiritual or worldly. There are a number of other concepts that are covered in the book, including the concept of the half-truth, covered in Chapter 5; Scarcity mindset, covered in Chapter 7; the concept that there really is no "good" and "evil" outside of my perception of what I like and don't like, covered in Chapter 9; and M. Scott Peck MD's 4-stage model of spiritual growth, covered in chapter 10.

Paul McKinley

The topic in *The Rules of the Spirit* that has really seemed to strike a chord with so many people is the discussion of forgiveness and apology from Chapter 4. It seems that most of the people I've met have a hard time with forgiving. After all, the World says you can use forgiveness as a carrot – *and* a stick – to get people to do what you want. The problem with the worldly view of forgiveness is, after all, that we are all spirits having a human experience, and at some level this concept of the role of forgiveness simply does not feel right. It does not resonate with truth. It's possible, of course, to wallow in the cesspool of unforgiveness to the extent that this lack of resonance or dissonance is drowned out. But in the still, quiet times the sensation is still there. At some level you know it's *not* the truth, and you know that you know.

So we begin our examination of forgiveness. In order to do that, we need to review some of the information presented in *The Rules of the Spirit* so that you will understand the "Rules" paradigm, which paves the way for the rest of the book.

I will mention that I write from the perspective of my Christian tradition. However, I consider myself to be a "spiritualist," not a "religionist." I believe that a focus on spiritual truths will always lead to the highest good regardless of the spiritual tradition. Therefore I invite you, the reader, to translate the concepts and ideas presented in this book into the "language" of your own spiritual tradition. If the concepts and ideas I present contain truth, and if you can look past the language I use to present them, the truth will become evident to you and you may achieve enlightenment that you might not otherwise. It won't matter whether you align yourself with Christian, Muslim, Buddhist, Hindu, or any other spiritual tradition.

In The World, Not Of The World.

A number of years ago I became intrigued by the phrase "We are in the world, but not of the world." This is a pretty common saying; I would expect that most people who follow mainstream Christian traditions would recognize the phrase. I believe the concept is pervasive in other traditions as well.

The dichotomy of this phrase begs the question: if we are IN the world, but not OF the world, then where - or what - ARE we OF? What does it mean to be NOT of the world? These questions became the seed for a new paradigm and understanding for living a discerning, spiritual life, which is described in this book. I am referring to is my "Rules of the Spirit" or "Rules" paradigm.

If we are IN the world, but not OF the world, where are we OF? My answer to this question is that we are of SPIRIT – we are Spirit beings, not Material. Pinch your arm. Does that substance you feel between your fingers define what or who you really are? I would say no, that is just a construct, a creation. This answer is based on my understanding of life, which is, of course, based on my experiences.

As I continued to think about this phrase and what it means, I began to recognize that, while we live our lives in the material world, the world can have an influence on the way we behave, which may or may not line up with our true, spiritual existence. It also challenged my understanding of Reality. Richard Bach used the analogy of a movie theater for describing our material existence. When you go to see a movie, you go into the theater, sit down and, for the moment, put aside your own reality for the fictional reality of the movie. You feel the excitement and pain of the characters on the screen; the images become real. After a while the movie is over, the lights come up and you wipe the matter from your eyes and file out to rejoin the "real" world waiting for you outside. It seems to me that life is like that – we forget for the brief moment of a lifetime about who we really are. The laws that apply to the fictional storyline have little to do with our basic reality.

Exploring the Origins

I asked Rev. David Adkins, who at the time was Senior Pastor of First United Methodist Church in Round Rock TX, if he knew where the "in the world, not of the world" phrase came from. His response was that "It sounds kinda Ephesiany." I tried to look up the phrase in various digital versions of the Bible, and although I found verses similar to it, there was no match. There are verses where Jesus refers to himself and his disciples as being "not of this world." There are also verses attributed to the Apostle Paul that refer to living "in the world." My current understanding is that this phrase is traditional liturgy that was in common practice in the 19th century, which means it was used in worship services and prayers as well as statements of faith. While it is not a scriptural quote, it is a paraphrase of scripture – a condensing of a concept that runs through the Protestant Christian New Testament. It is a common phrase in the Christian mindshare. It is used in Christian teaching to encourage the spiritual student to examine their thoughts and behaviors in a different context than the habitual pattern of the world around them. It encourages conscious living, and, to a degree, conscious living based on an example.

What does it say about *who we are*?

What meaning does the phrase "In the world, but not of the world" have with respect to *who we are*? Frankly, the saying could have any number of meanings. An agnostic or atheist might interpret it to mean that we are descended from an alien race. That might be interesting! I believe the more common interpretation is, as I mentioned earlier, that we are of Spirit - expatriot aliens or not. Our real nature is of a substance or character that cannot be measured or quantified in the material world. The laws of the material world don't apply to us, or at least they apply only to the extent that we allow them. In fact it has been my observation that space and time have no meaning in Spirit. I read somewhere that it had been proven that "energy" healing methodologies are not constrained by the speed of light - that whatever is done in one location is instantly manifested in another without the delay that would normally be associated with the "laws of physics" as we know them. Distance also has no effect either, in time or in effectiveness. It doesn't matter whether the person being treated is in the same room as the healer, or miles or worlds away. There is a good example of this in the biblical story of the Centurion who came to Jesus seeking healing for his servant. The servant "was healed at that moment" without Jesus having to go to the centurion's home or wherever the servant was located. It didn't matter where the servant was.

What does it say about how we could live?

The thing that's really interesting about being NOT *of the world* is that it suggests that there is a whole different way of thinking about the way we live. Just as Spirit is not held to the "laws" of physics, so also could the way we live, the way we think, and the way we interact with one another be based on an entirely different set of rules and concepts. The laws of physics appear from a worldly view to be immutable, meaning that they apply in all circumstances. However I have already shown how they do not apply to Spirit action: the laws of physics are true for the world, but they are not true for Spirit. What else of what we believe and accept from the world does not apply to Spirit? How do Spirit rules apply in worldly situations? When there is a conflict between the ways and methods of the world and the ways and methods of the Spirit, which one wins out? How do we decide what is worldly and what is of the Spirit? How do we begin to integrate these truths into how we live, and what is the outcome if we do? What is the incentive for adopting this way of thinking and behaving?

What does it say about our future?

We all know that each of us will pass away from this life at some point. If the spiritual life is real, if we are truly *of the Spirit*, it follows that we will return to that realm. All of the things that pertain to the world will become of no consequence – because they weren't ever really "real."

If the World's viewpoint isn't real, then how did we fall into a state of subscribing to a whole set of beliefs that aren't really real? I mention in *The Rules of the Spirit* Chapter 7, the story of Adam and Eve, which I believe to be the metaphorical story of how mankind came to imbibe or "take in" the concept of *good* and *evil*, of *abundance* and *scarcity*. Before the "fall," mankind, through Adam and Eve, had no concept of *evil*, but only of *good*. They had no concept of *scarcity*. But through absorbing these concepts, which are false concepts by the way, it has colored the mindset and behavior of mankind ever since. It's like a virus that, once contracted, can never be fully eliminated from the body. Once Pandora's box has been opened, the evils cannot be put back.

Due to the presence of the Law of Attraction, if you hold the concept of scarcity in your mindset, then scarcity is what you will manifest, or produce in your environment. So, it's like a self-fulfilling prophesy. If you think about scarcity, if you fear scarcity, if you put a great deal of energy into scarcity by trying to avoid it, what do you get? More scarcity!

Good and evil are somewhat similar to scarcity and abundance, except that good and evil aren't something you create; they are really just a reflection of your perception. Things you like or approve are "*good*," while things you don't like are "*evil*." The same Law of Attraction applies, however: as you put energy into labeling something as evil, as you rail against what is evil, as you feel the strong negative emotions about that which you judge to be evil, guess what? You are creating more things and circumstances in your life that you will perceive to be "evil." I discussed more deeply the topic of good and evil in *The Rules of the Spirit* so that you can better understand the concept that good and evil are perception-based.

The bottom line, though, is that over the millennia, as humankind has come to better understand our spiritual roots, we are moving more and more back towards an Eden life. It may seem to you that there are a lot of evil (there's that perception again) things happening in the contemporary world. However, if you compare life as we know it today to that of a thousand, or two or three thousand years ago, it's possible to see how we as mankind have progressed. Two hundred years ago, slavery was commonplace, while today it is considered criminal. Two thousand years ago crucifixion was a common means of executing someone. Today we're moving towards a concept that execution *in and of itself* is *never* appropriate. If you look for them, there are many other indications that mankind is evolving toward a more spiritual existence in the worldly environment. It may be that the evils cannot be put back into Pandora's box, but we can learn to understand them and tame them; to overcome them. We can learn to understand that all things God created, including the things that were created through God's creation of Mankind, are good and have blessings, even if we choose not to enjoy them much.

Go to http://theenergyofforgiveness.com/chapter-1 for additional material.

Chapter 2
The "Rules" Paradigm

"Enjoy the little things, for one day you may look back and realize they were the big things."
— Robert Brault

World Vs Spirit

My answer, as I've said, to the "where ARE we of" question is that we are of Spirit. I've also heard the phrase "We are spirits having a human experience, not humans having a spiritual experience." So, that's great. We are of the Spirit. So what? What does that mean? What is its significance? What does that say about our reality?

Maybe I should define here what I mean by "Spirit." Webster defines spirit as "an animating or vital principle held to give life to physical organisms" or "a supernatural being or essence" among other definitions. I use the word Spirit in several contexts. When I use Spirit as a proper noun, I am referring to a universal "essence," as Webster puts it; the timeless and unmeasurable part of who I am; of who we are.

The source of Spirit is God, so that means we are of God. We are the children of God, many Christians would say, although they would also almost in the same breath deny their inheritance. For instance, modern Christians don't really believe that "miraculous" healings can take place in this day and age. If I demonstrate such a miraculous healing by helping someone get rid of their headache using Reiki, they would instantly label it as "of Satan" and freak out about it in fear. What is it with modern religion that teaches if you don't understand it, it must be feared? After all, Jesus himself said, "Greater things than these will you do," referring to his own miracles. Why is it that religion teaches us to fear? Spirituality has nothing to do with fear, as we'll explore later in this chapter.

If we are children of God, that means we would be imbued with the qualities of God. Genesis 1:26 says "Let us make humankind in our image, according to our likeness..." Does that mean God has ten fingers and ten toes? I think not! It's the *creative spirit* of God that we inherited. If we are to fully live our inheritance as children of God, it seems appropriate that we should live the qualities of God. These form what I believe are the truth to our reality – the "Rules" to live by.

Love

Let's start our exploration by asking what is God? Some would say that God is Love. If we use that as the primary quality, then Love becomes the primary "Rule" that applies to us as Spirit. What works for Spirit life is built on a foundation of Love. Many of the "Ten Commandments" embody that truth. Jesus said "'Love the

The Energy of Forgiveness

Lord your God with all your heart and with all your soul and with all your mind.' This is the first and greatest commandment. And the second is like it: 'Love your neighbor as yourself'. All the Law and the Prophets hang on these two commandments." (Matt 22:37 NIV). Love is the most basic characteristic of our spiritual nature.

What does Love mean? Modern English has come to use the word as being the same as an extreme level of "liking" something. If you look up the word love in the dictionary, you'll find any number of definitions, both noun and verb, that have nothing to do with Love – and likely none that do define Love. Someone might exclaim, "Oh, I love that sweater," but that's not Love. That's something called "cathecting." Many people mistake Love for the feeling of emotional attachment to a person or thing, but I promise you emotion has nothing to do with Love. People talk about "falling in love" or romantic love. I promise also that isn't Love. It's a chemical trick our bodies play on us. It feels really good in the moment, and causes pain when we do something or something happens that threatens that relationship, but it has nothing to do with Love. Love isn't something you *feel*. And it's not something you do for emotional reasons.

The word Love is a *verb* – it's something you *do*, not something you *feel*. It seems to me that I could live my life consistently acting out Love without ever experiencing the *feeling* most people associate with Love. For instance, as I pass through a day in my life, there are countless ways I can be loving to those around me, through holding a door, or complimenting something.

Paul McKinley

I don't have an emotional attachment to that person. I know nothing about them except what I can sense in the moment! I may feel good about doing whatever act I've chosen to do, but that's more a question of being satisfied that I am meeting my self-appointed goal of being a loving person.

Love can be acted out by simply smiling at someone. Dr. Paul Ekman found through research that not only does the face reveal the emotions a person is feeling, because emotions trigger specific groups of forty-three different facial muscles to contract, but by intentionally using those muscles the person may experience the emotion tied to the expression. It's also well known that people tend to "mirror" facial expressions. For instance if I smile at someone, they are likely to smile back. When they smile back, they will feel the emotion of happiness behind the smiling. They will feel better. So just smiling at people in everyday situations can be a very simple act of Love because it helps and encourages them to feel better.

Scott Peck, MD described Love as "the willingness to improve one's self for the benefit of another." I would define it as "the act of seeking and doing that which seems to serve the highest good." Keep in mind that as a human it's very difficult to discern the "highest good." It can take a lot of hard thought and soul-searching and you still may not get it "right." Also, we're not talking about pleasing the other person. Sometimes what serves the "highest good" can be unpleasant, which gives rise to the term "tough love."

Grace

I would say that the next most important quality of Spirit is Grace. What is Grace? What does the word Grace mean? My definition of Grace is the "living out of Love," a peaceful acceptance and responding to every situation in a way that reflects the highest good, as I understand it. It means unconditional love – that no matter what happens, love has always been there and will always be there. The relationship and the caring cannot be destroyed no matter what happens or how spectacular our mistakes. Grace means implicit acceptance of what is: to accept me as I am; to accept you as you are. Grace is the ultimate "willingness to allow beingness."

The worldly concept of "quid pro quo" or "this for that" has no meaning in the presence of Grace. It has no meaning in the reality of Spirit. Grace means "this without that" or "this, because it's the Loving thing to do; the act that serves the highest good." The "this for that" concept is what I call "transactional" mindset. Grace has no concept of a transaction or contract. Grace works in terms of covenants. A covenant is a one-sided agreement where one party agrees to do something for another, with no requirement or expectation from the second party. Anytime you see something that follows the "this for that" mindset, you can be assured that it is a worldly thing, not Spirit based. "This for that" is a scarcity mindset concept. Basically scarcity mindset is saying that I have to maintain balance, because if I give without expecting return I will become depleted – my needs will not be met. But scarcity is a worldly concept. Spirit has only a concept of Abundance, which says that whatever

I need will be automatically created for me out of the unlimitedness of Spirit energy! So Spirit does not *need* to seek compensation. Spirit is free to demonstrate Grace.

One of the things I was taught in my Reiki classes is not to use my own energy in a treatment. For one thing, my energy is not appropriate for the person receiving the treatment. But the main thing is that by using my own energy I am depleting it. The proper way is to channel the energy from Spirit, which is limitless and wholeness. This is how Abundance works: receiving from Spirit whatever is needed.

The dictionary definition of grace is "the free and unmerited favor of God." In other words, I don't need to *do anything* to receive the gifts of Spirit. That's about the best description of Grace I can give. Grace is serving the highest good, in all situations, regardless of the past or the future (remember time has no meaning in Spirit).

Trust

Finally, the third quality is Trust. Trust means that I know you will do the best you can in any situation. And that's the truth of it – that we all do the best we can in the moment, all things considered. Spiritual-based trust takes that into account. It doesn't depend on the other person agreeing to the Spiritual ruleset. True Trust is just as unconditional as true Love. Trust says that I'm going to accept you and love you no matter what your choices are. That is unconditional love. This is the basis of Covenant – the one-sided promise. God trusts us to do the best we can. I believe that's part of why you don't see "divine intervention" on a regular basis. This is also a large part of the lesson that Jesus teaches us in his willingness to be sacrificed. By being willing to be sacrificed, He demonstrated trust in God – that life isn't the all-in-all; that as a spirit he was safe and nothing truly harmful – in a spiritual sense – could possibly happen to him.

Imagine a parent that doesn't trust their child in anything, but rather pushes them out of the way to do whatever needs to be done in every activity. This isn't very healthy. Where is the opportunity for the child to learn and grow on their own? They will remain helpless as long as they are not given the opportunity to make a few mistakes and learn from the experience for themselves. The role of a parent is to work themselves out of a job. In order for a child to become a healthy, happy adult, they must be given opportunities to learn, and to experience the result of that learning. They won't be able to do that if the parent is hovering over them, doing everything for them, and preventing them from doing anything for themselves because they "might break it" or "might get hurt."

Now, imagine an environment where it is impossible for the "child" to be damaged in any way – the ultimate "sandbox." They are surrounded by loving "elders" and are given access to whatever knowledge they seek and can do whatever they want without fear. They can experience pain or pleasure. They can create whatever they want. The role of the "elders" is to assist and encourage, but only assistance and encouragement as is asked for by the "child." They can throw sand and observe the consequences. It is a learning, creating experience with nothing to fear, no permanent negative results. The freedom of experience leads to further creation based on the experience. This is how I perceive the mortal existence. The things we get so wrapped up about really have little significance in the spiritual sense. It's all good!

Fear

Now that we've explored the Spirit side, let's look at the other side of this dichotomy: the World. The World in most ways is the opposite or diametrically opposed to the ways of the Spirit. Take the first quality of Spirit: Love. There are many opinions about what is the opposite of Love. The one that seems to best fit this "Rules" paradigm is that the opposite of Love is FEAR. The Worldly way is the way of Fear. Because we've "bought into" (or been indoctrinated into) the ways of the world, we live in Fear and we live out of Fear, meaning that much of our behavior is built on a foundation of Fear. Anger is always built on a foundation of fear. Scarcity mindset is based in fear. The prevalence of fear in our experience is part of the inheritance from Adam and Eve, which I covered in *The Rules of the Spirit* Chapter 7.

I believe babies do not experience fear when they are newborn. They are not born in fear. They definitely have likes and dislikes in the moment, which they will let you know about in no uncertain terms. They also may have a natural reaction to a certain stimulus such as falling. But they don't have fear. They *learn* to fear. Fear is not *natural* to them. Fear is a worldly thing, and they've just come fresh from Spirit, which has no concept of fear. You can see this play out in a kitten who also seems to have no fear and will 'attack' a large dog.

The Energy of Forgiveness

Fear drives out intelligence. When you slip into fear, you are unable to use the intelligence you have to make rational decisions, so a decision you make in fear, if you could call it a decision, is much less likely to serve your own good, and even less the highest good. Fear is really good at getting you to jump, but the jump is just as likely to be from the frying pan into the fire as it is to safety. Fear is also just as likely to cause you to freeze. The decision to jump or to freeze is not a measured decision. Fear is not very good at getting us to a better place.

An environment of fear leads us to try to fulfill our own needs and desires rather than looking to the highest good. We learn to use Fear as a means of getting what we want. Because we live in Fear, we feel the need to control our environment. We must control our circumstances as well as the people around us, because if we don't, our fears will become realized. Control becomes the second rule of the World. One must Control in order to deal with or avoid the Fear.

Control & Power

The opposite of Grace is Power. Grace means "Willingly, free and unmerited, because it's the right thing to do." Power says "because I'm stronger than you and I can make you." Negotiation can be a form of exercising power. If you can find out what I really want or what my other circumstances are, you can leverage that knowledge to gain power over me and get a better deal for yourself, at my expense. You fill the need to address your scarcity by creating more scarcity for me. You could say that I freely agreed to the transaction, when my agreement is under duress.

Paul McKinley

The opposite of Trust is Control. If you don't trust someone to do something you want them to do, then you are going to feel a need to Control them. If you don't trust circumstances to provide what you need, then you're going to feel a need to Control your circumstances rather than letting it happen in the natural flow of things. "This for that" is a form of controlling another – getting someone else to do what you want.

The challenge here is that we all fear something, we're all attempting to Control our circumstances, and as long as we're living in and out of Fear, our needs, wants, and fears often conflict. The felt need to control becomes a power play between individuals or groups of individuals. If what I want and what you want conflict, then we get into an ante-up race of who can control the other in order to get what they want.

The one who has the most Power in the circumstance wins, the other loses. Whoever has the most Power gets what they want. It's always a win-lose situation. The idea of win-lose is a very basic worldly concept that has no meaning in the spiritual realm. Spirit only knows win-win that serves the highest good. Anything less than win-win means that *both* sides lose something. There is a saying that "power corrupts, and absolute power corrupts absolutely." This corruption is because Power becomes the final blow to our connection to our spiritual reality. It's what pushes us over the edge into the insanity of the material or worldly mindset, so the more powerful we become in the worldly sense, the more our connection with *who we really are* is broken. When we are disconnected with who we are, we are living in unreality; we are spiritually insane.

The Energy of Forgiveness

Rules in a Nutshell

So, here are the Rules in a nutshell, in the form of a diagram for the "Rules" paradigm. The Rules of the World are listed on the left, and The Rules of the Spirit are on the right. I often refer to the Rules of the World as "Control-Power-Fear."

World	Spirit
Fear	Love
Power	Grace
Control	Trust

An interesting, and I think really crucial, observation that I've had about the "Rules" paradigm is that the Rules of the World only *seem* to work, while The Rules of the Spirit actually do work, *always*. I believe this is because the Spirit is the reality, while the World is the illusion, the dream-world, the insanity.

If you think about it, you'll realize this is true. You may be able to get what you want from someone through intimidation (Fear), but the result will always be somewhat unpredictable and may not be what you wanted at all. The beaten dog may slink away, but it may also turn around and tear your throat out. Fear only has the appearance of working. I mentioned earlier about fear driving away intelligence, so it's not surprising that a response gained from creating fear will tend to be unpredictable. Fear is also a "Fight or Flight" type thing, so if what you're trying to achieve doesn't fit those two responses, the response is not likely to be what you want.

Paul McKinley

It's been well understood over the ages that people will do things for Love that they would not do for Fear. Love is often the motivator that leads individuals to overcome their fear and do things that we marvel at as heroic, even to the point of death. This is borne out in scripture: "Perfect love casts out all fear" (1 John 4:18) and "Greater love has no one than this, than to lay down one's life for his friends" (John 15:13). Love is more powerful than Fear. My observation is that way of Love – the way of Spirit – always works. It is the real Reality. It is the Truth. If I can train myself out of the Worldly indoctrination and live totally by Love, Grace, and Trust, I will always receive what I need, my relationships will be healthy, and I will enjoy life to its fullest.

Our willingness to do things out of Love that overpowers Fear is Truth, but it is also our spiritual heritage, like inheriting crooked toes or blue eyes from our parents.

I find that by understanding this "Rules" paradigm, it helps me to recognize worldly habits and actions, both in myself and others. I'm not responsible for the way others behave, of course, but as I identify the worldly habits and actions in myself, I can begin to act on them, and replace them with acts based in Spirit. As I really begin to understand how to act in the Truth of the likeness of Spirit, I then begin to improve my own life. As I become more spiritual, I am happier, and those around me are happier. They also notice the difference, and some are challenged to work on adopting the same mindshare and behaviors in their own lives.

The Half-Truth

Another interesting observation that comes out of the "Rules" paradigm has to do with Truth. One might expect that the Spiritual realm would be characterized by Truth; there's no surprise here.

The assumption, however, might be that the World would be characterized not by Truth, but by lack of truth. There would be no surprise there either, except that's not been my observation. On the contrary, what I've noticed is that the way of the World is not lack of Truth but rather what I call the Half-Truth, meaning there is truth mixed with non-truth, or only partial truth rather than the whole truth. And, more often than not, the Half-Truth results in the Reality Inversion I mentioned earlier. It's a very curious and interesting phenomenon.

I think the reason the World deals in Half-Truths (rather than pure untruth) is because people generally recognize things that are blatantly false. If I tell you something that is patently untrue, you would reject what I'd told you straightaway. But if I couch the lie as a portion of a greater truth, it's not so clear anymore. The 1960's film "Mary Poppins" popularized the song "A Spoonful of Sugar Makes the Medicine Go Down." And so it is with Truth, for our minds which are clouded by the Worldly insanity: a spoonful of truth makes the untruth go down, "in the most delightful way," if you'll pardon my ironic continuation of the lyric.

And down it goes quite well. It's not falseness if it contains the truth, is it? You're walking along just fine down the path of truth, and suddenly you're not in truth anymore. Except that oftentimes, if not most of the time, you don't notice that you've veered off the path. You just notice that things become difficult. I'm reminded of a scene in Tolkien's "Lord of the Rings" series where the band of dwarves strayed off the elven path through Mirkwood by becoming enchanted by mysterious lights. Once off the path they can't find their way back and are only saved by being captured by the elves. So is it with the half-truth; you become enchanted by the parts that are truth, and once off the path you don't even really recognize that you're lost.

One thing I've also noticed is that once people have bought into or as I say "imbibed" the Half-Truth, they will defend it to the death. In modern vernacular one might say they have "drunk the Kool-Aid." After all, if I admit that I've swallowed a Half-Truth, I'm also admitting that I've been duped, that I'm stupid and foolish and can't tell the truth from untruth. I'm admitting that I've done something wrong, and this puts me out of Control, which is a *bad place to be* in a world characterized by Control-Power-Fear. Not good! This must be avoided at all costs! I think maybe the way to produce the most vigorous defensive effort from a person or group of people is to arrange for their half-truth to be challenged.

Be sure to check http://theenergyofforgiveness.com/chapter-2 for additional material.

Chapter 3
The Reality Inversion

"In quarreling, the truth is always lost."
— *Publilius Syrus*

Forgiveness and Apology

Another interesting phenomenon that the "Rules" paradigm helps us to understand is that the Rules of the World twist spiritual concepts or Truths to be the exact opposite of what they truly are. This is what I call a "Reality Inversion." It's not that reality is really inverted, but rather that our *perception* of reality is upside-down or backwards.

I remember reading about an experiment that was performed using special goggles that invert the visual image so that for the wearer of the goggles everything appeared to be upside-down. During the first four days nothing remarkable happened. The images seemed inverted, and as soon as the goggles were removed everything was right again. On the fifth day, however, the images appeared upright again when the goggles were being worn. Taking the goggles off resulted in the images being inverted again. The brain had adapted to the inversion and taken the inverted image as now "normal." In much the same way, we have taken as "normal" the "inverted" perception that the Worldly mindset presents.

Forgiveness and apology is one of the best examples of this "Reality Inversion" because our whole concept of the purpose and function of forgiveness and apology is inverted. For instance, if I do something that harms you, the World says I "owe" you an apology, and you may or may not "forgive" me for this event, holding the forgiveness over my head as something I must earn. This is actually the exact opposite of the truth: forgiveness is for the forgiver, and apology is for the apologetic.

Does this seem strange to you? Let's examine this concept. Take for example a psychopathic criminal. Does it do the psychopath any good to forgive them for their crime? They are likely not mentally capable of recognizing what they've done, or even that they have or have not been forgiven. What effect does it have on them whether they are forgiven? Nothing! They don't care, nor are they capable of understanding it, so it has no effect on them whatsoever. Does withholding forgiveness undo the crime? Even if they were sorry for their deed, would it change the reality of the harm done? It would not. This is true for the mentally competent as well. Does giving or withholding forgiveness change *what is* or erase the harm? Of course not!

On the other hand, look at the effect on the person who has suffered the harm. By harboring the bitterness, hurt, anger and hatred towards the criminal, they only bring themselves additional harm. Do you really enjoy being bitter or angry? Some people do, but that's their own neurosis/psychosis. Ask your physician what effect hard emotions like bitterness, anger, or hatred have on your health and you'll probably get an earful: high blood pressure, autoimmune diseases, maybe even cancer. I believe it was Buddha who said, "Refusing to forgive is like drinking a poison and expecting the other person to die." That's one of my favorite quotes. For me it is right up there with any quote from Ralph Waldo Emerson.

Let's look at a special case: when the one you need to forgive is someone who deeply and genuinely cares about you and regrets what has happened. Refusing to forgive in this situation is not only abusive to yourself because of the damage from negative emotions, but it is also creating harm for the other person. Through unforgiveness, *you* are becoming the transgressor. Carried to an extreme, you may even destroy the relationship with that person. I have news for you; if you destroy the relationships with the people who care deeply about you, you will live a very unhappy life! You will have harmed yourself to an extreme!

Do you enjoy being around people who are bitter or angry? You may understand why they're bitter, but it doesn't make it pleasant. Often people who are acting out of bitterness bring themselves more bitterness by alienating those around them. Their bitterness leads people around them to do things in a way that is, shall we say, less than optimal. It's a vicious cycle: bitterness and negative emotion breeds bitterness and negative emotion in those around us, as well as creating situations that bring us more bitterness and negativity. Bitterness and negativity attracts more bitterness and negativity – on more than one level, as we'll explore in Chapter 8 and Chapter 9.

What is the sense in withholding forgiveness when it only harms yourself? This is why Jesus counseled Peter to forgive "even seventy times seven." By the way, "seventy times seven" in this context does not mean 490 times or even "a great many times." The symbology of the numbers means something like "until the forgiveness is perfect and whole" or in more modern language "whatever it takes."

Apology

The flip side of forgiveness is apology. What is apology? It is the acknowledgement of our own action and responsibility in an event. What role does it play? The fact is that we cannot control our own behavior unless we can recognize what we are doing and take ownership of it. It's not uncommon these days to see one person harm another, and then blame any scapegoat imaginable, up to and including the person they've harmed. Western society has a widespread psychosis of seeking to blame first rather than look within. It's always someone else's or something else's fault, never our own. My own country, the United States, is particularly bad about this, which leads it to be the most litigious (lawsuit-happy) society in the world. This attitude is illustrated in the cartoon character Bart Simpson's common phrase "I didn't do it" which he pops out any time he feels attention is moving in his direction.

The Energy of Forgiveness

By abdicating responsibility for our actions and refusing to look within, we cripple ourselves. We can really only control ourselves, we are really only responsible for ourselves. If we refuse to look to, and live out of, our selves (note the distinction "our *selves*"), well that's just insane. It places impossible expectations on ourselves and others. That is a recipe for failure. Conscious living requires introspection. It means considering my actions and their potential outcomes, so that I don't carelessly harm those around me.

The fact is that whether or not you take responsibility for your deed, you still suffer from the deed yourself. If you're always carelessly stepping on other people's toes, you may wonder why people are avoiding you or are treating you poorly. If you are habitually careless about how your actions affect others, like the cartoon character Bart Simpson, it will always be you that people suspect. Only when you recognize what you are doing can you begin to observe yourself and work on changing your behavior. This is the real role of apology: to really take ownership of your own actions so that you can begin to change your behavior and grow spiritually – to reclaim your spiritual inheritance by learning to act out of Love.

Do you ever "owe" someone an apology? No! Well, maybe I should qualify that. The only one that you "owe" an apology to is yourself. Mind you, you may actually be apologizing to someone else, but the benefit of the apology falls to you, not them. You owe it to yourself, *not them*. You owe it to yourself to apologize, because only through apologizing do you really internalize ownership and responsibility for whatever has happened. Only through ownership can you begin to change.

It may be that you cannot actually apologize to the other person. They may have passed on, or they may be too upset with you to accept your apology, or they may have otherwise passed out of your reach. That doesn't matter. You don't own their situation or emotions. Just do the apology! Write them a letter, even if you burn it afterwards. Go look in the mirror and apologize to them – because you're really apologizing for your own benefit. Just do it! Remember that it's through your acknowledging your part in the event that the benefit comes. Until you do, you're carrying around that baggage, and it will weigh on you until you let it go.

Rules applied to Forgiveness and Apology

Let's look at forgiveness/apology from another perspective. If I've done something to harm you and I truly give a hoot about whether you forgive me or not, that indicates that I care about the relationship and have already taken ownership of the deed. Withholding forgiveness in this case is reduced to a power-play. It is a way of manipulating someone who's made a poor choice or had an accident. It's a "Control-Power-Fear" thing, rooted in the World, disconnected from Spirit.

If you think about it, it's really a bit of cruelty. Let's say I did something that harmed you, but I've acknowledged my part though apology and done the best I can to make it good, recognizing that some harms cannot be put right. At that point, holding the grudge is just rubbing my nose in it. I've done the best I can - there's nothing else I can do. It's just a question of you holding on to the hurtness, and then using that hurtness as a justification for your own aggression. Now you are the aggressor. This is not healthy. It's not healthy for me, it's not healthy for you, and it's destructive to the relationship.

An enlightened understanding of being forgiven is that I might desire your forgiveness, not for my sake but because I understand the effect that lack of forgiveness has on you. My wish for forgiveness is not about wanting to be forgiven myself; it is vested in my wish for your wellbeing, and has nothing to do with me. This is an attitude based in Love – seeking always the Highest Good. For example, once when Ann was working one-on-one with a colleague, they had an argument about a project she was responsible for. The colleague stormed out of the room slamming the door. Ann made a point of making herself available throughout the day, deliberately working close to him because she knew he needed to apologize. He did before the end of the day! She had already forgiven him but she knew he needed to come clean on his side for him to feel better.

Self-Forgiveness

Self-forgiveness is probably the most important aspect of forgiveness. One of the important things that people need to understand is that if you can't forgive someone else, you also cannot forgive yourself. After all, we've all made mistakes. We've all done things we wish we hadn't. If we find it difficult to forgive others, then we know that at some point there's the difficulty in forgiving ourselves. Christians are familiar with the Lord's Prayer, which includes the phrase: "Forgive us our debts, as we forgive our debtors." The typical focus is "Forgive US our debts" but the second part is more important: "as we forgive our debtors." Somewhere down in your conscious or subconscious mind you know that if you're not forgiving others, basically the prayer is saying "I don't forgive others, so don't forgive me either." My subconscious perception of my own deservingness of forgiveness is based on whether I forgive, so if I don't forgive others I'm saying to myself that *I* cannot be forgiven. That's really tough to see yourself as undeserving of forgiveness. There's no way out of that rathole!

Forgiving ourselves is just as important as forgiving someone else. If refusing to forgive is like taking a poison and expecting the other person to get sick, what about when YOU are the other person? That's the only way that the poison is effective! It's guaranteed to cause problems! All sorts of illnesses result from lack of self-forgiveness. It's easy to push down the thoughts of self-forgiveness, to put it off or to avoid confronting the self-forgiveness issue, but the issue remains and it affects the things you see showing up. The lack of forgiveness is eating away at you every minute of every day. It's destroying your health. It's causing you to react to situations in ways that aren't beneficial to you, in ways that do not serve the highest good. So, Self-forgiveness is maybe even more important than forgiving someone else.

Self-forgiveness can often be more difficult than forgiving someone else. Why is that? For one thing you may tend to deny that you've done something that needs forgiveness. Another reason is that you probably hold yourself to a higher standard than others. The fact of the matter is that you are human, and just as subject to making mistakes as anyone else. We are all the same in that way. Holding yourself to the higher standard where mistakes are not acceptable means that when you do make mistakes, those mistakes become figurative rocks in your knapsack that you have to carry with you wherever you go, weighing you down, distorting your posture and sapping your strength. The only solution is to learn to be loving of yourself and to forgive yourself – as you forgive others.

Judas Story

The Judas story is a good example of *lack* of *self-forgiveness*. One of the messages that I've given many times is the "other side" of the Judas story. I call it "The Saddest Story in the Bible" or "The Hardest One to Forgive." It's a good message for the Sunday after Easter.

It's common knowledge in Christian tradition that Judas was the one who betrayed Jesus. Judas is the one that everyone loves to hate. But there's another side to this story. There was a sect in Jesus' time called Zealots, who believed that the Messiah would be a military leader who would free the Hebrew people from Roman rule. Judas was not described as a zealot, but one of the other disciples was. Let's assume for the moment that Judas was of like mind to the Zealots. He clearly believed that Jesus was the Messiah as he'd been accompanying Jesus for several years. He'd heard the wisdom and seen the miracles. He probably thought he was going to be one of the patriarchs of twelve new tribes of Israel. He was ready for the challenge! But then Jesus started talking crazy stuff about going away! Mary anointed Jesus with nard, an expensive perfume used to dress people who have died. I'm sure the symbolism was not lost on Judas.

So, Judas decides he's going to take matters into his own hands by forcing Jesus to take action. He goes and works out a deal with the leadership to hand Jesus over to them, thinking that would force Jesus to "start the revolution." But then things don't go quite according to plan. Instead of coming out fighting, Jesus heals the guard that Peter had injured and goes away peacefully. He then allows himself to be tortured and killed. Judas, thinking that he's caused Jesus' murder, kills himself. This is the part I refer to as being "the saddest story in the Bible." If you understand the story from this context, you begin to understand just a little bit of the anguish that Judas must have felt. From the point where he tries to return the money, his world comes crashing down on him and there's nothing he can do about it. Jesus himself said, "It would be better for him if he had not been born." I don't believe that was condemnation, but rather empathy for how he knew Judas would feel after the fact.

The thing to remember about this story is that Jesus had already forgiven Judas, even telling him "do it now." What Judas did had to be done according to prophesy, and who knows how things would have turned out otherwise. Only through the crucifixion and resurrection could Jesus have demonstrated his mastery, to show us that we need not fear death, that we could endure even an agonizing death at the hands of others and still be willing to forgive. How different the story might have been, had Judas been able to forgive himself and had not killed himself. How would it have been, had Judas been there when Jesus appeared in the Upper Room? Jesus invited doubting Thomas to put his finger in the wound in Jesus' side; would he also have assured Judas of his forgiveness and explained to the others how Judas had played a part that *nobody* would have wanted to play?

Half-truth in Forgiveness and Apology

Let's look at the Half-Truth as it applies to the forgiveness/apology Reality Inversion. Both the World and the Spirit say that forgiveness and apology are valuable, even crucial. As I've mentioned, the reality of Spirit is that the benefit of forgiveness goes to the forgiver, and apology benefits the apologist. That's the Truth, and it's based in Love, a characteristic of the Spirit. By switching or "inverting" the supposed beneficiaries, the World makes the forgiveness/apology into a Control-Power-Fear thing. That little switch, the little half-truth of who benefits, corrupts the whole understanding. The truth part of it is that forgiveness is needed, and apology is needed. Both are important. The untruth part of it is buried down in the fine print where it defines who are the beneficiaries.

Conveniently the corruption works in a way that plays into the hand of control-power-fear. Instead of forgiving for my own benefit – no power to control someone else there – I can hold the forgiveness over your head to get you to do something I want or otherwise control you. I can even beat you over the head with it by making sure you never forget how you've harmed me, reusing over and over the same possibly trivial error to exercise my power. There's no telling how long I can keep up this control I have over you by refusing to forgive. Keep in mind that this only works because basically everyone alive has bought into the Worldly mindset and the Worldly concept of forgiveness and apology, so they believe that they need something from you: your forgiveness.

Let's take the forgiveness/apology thing a bit further. I have observed earlier that if a person can't forgive others, they can't forgive themselves either. We've all done things we aren't proud of. We've all done things that harm either ourselves or others. I believe that even extremely narcissistic people understand at some level that they have done things that were harmful to others.

Whenever you find yourself unwilling to forgive another, at some point deep down, maybe so deep it's at the unconscious level, you're saying to yourself "if they don't deserve forgiveness for that deed, then how does my deed compare? At what point does a deed become 'forgivable' or 'not forgivable'?" I may think to myself "I'd never do something as horrible as HE did." And maybe I wouldn't do exactly the same thing. But I might have done something else that was equally as bad. Or, say, maybe half as bad. If something is half as bad, does that make it excusable? What fraction of something "bad" makes it "not bad"? Somewhere deep down, I know it doesn't matter – I know that I've done things I shouldn't. So for me to refuse forgiveness to another based on my own judgment of greater or lesser evil just doesn't hold water. At some level I will not be able to forgive myself either.

The Energy of Forgiveness

Actually, as I'll discuss later, self-forgiveness is often the hardest to do.

And so not only does the poison of negative emotion, resulting from refusing to forgive another, fester within you, it adds to all the negative things you've done in your own life. The venom you hold for others adds to the venom you hold for yourself. Things get pretty toxic. Eventually the toxins result in disease: cancer, arthritis (an auto-immune disease, basically self-destructive) or whatever. I'll discuss that later in this book, too.

Is it clear how unforgiveness only hurts yourself?

More material is available at http://theenergyofforgiveness.com/chapter-3.

Chapter 4
The Origins Of Forgiveness

"All you have to do is look hard enough. And what might seem to be a series of unfortunate events may in fact be the first steps of a journey."
— Daniel Handler, through the character of Lemony Snicket

The Root of Forgiveness

The word forgive is a verb, meaning it is an action. It's something that you do. But it's not something you just do "out of the blue" like flying a kite just because you feel like it. As we've just examined in Chapter 3 there is a need for forgiveness. So it's something you do to address a felt need, like the need to reduce pain by removing a splinter in your hand or the need to scratch an itch. That need is precipitated by a specific event. *There's always an event that precedes and originates the need for forgiveness.* There's something about the event that creates negative emotions - negative energy, or "bad vibes" as it was called in the 1970s. The negative emotion created by the event in turn creates the need for a release of the negative emotion; the destructive energy or tension. The need is for forgiveness.

Think about the things in your life that you feel badly about. Are you angry with someone? Ask yourself this question: "why am I angry with this person?" You may say it's because they did such-and-such, in which case there you have it: the such-and-such that they did is the event. If you just don't like them, dig a little deeper. I believe you'll find that there is some event or series of events that precipitated your dislike, such as they're always talking too loudly, or you hear them gossiping all the time.

I have a pretty finely-tuned sixth sense I call my "sleaze-meter." It's about 90 percent accurate. When I meet or even just see someone in a picture or whatever, my sleaze-meter either registers that this person is okay – they are genuine and trustworthy – or maybe they are in the "rubber glove" region, meaning I perceive them to be sleazy enough that I have the urge to put on rubber gloves to protect myself, or I might say they "peg" my sleaze-meter. The point here is that the "event" that may need to be forgiven is my perception – the *event* of my perception – that they have some degree of sleaziness. Even if they are, in fact, sleazy, I may have the need to forgive them for being sleazy – or even forgive myself for making that judgment about them especially when I don't know them at all. That doesn't mean I expose myself to their sleaziness, just that I don't allow my judgment of their character to fester negativity in *my* life.

The Event

There's an endless array of events that can precipitate the need for forgiveness. It could be your favorite vase was broken. It could be a mess was created, or something

The Energy of Forgiveness

that happened while you're driving, like someone pulling too close in front of you or cutting you off. It could be that you are prevented from doing something you wanted or needed to do. It could be something that just happens – an act of God you might call it, like a thunderstorm, tornado, earthquake, or a tree falling over.

It could be the threat of an event. In this case it's not the event that is threatened because the event hasn't happened. Rather the threat itself is the event. If someone pulls in front of you too closely when you're driving, the threat is that they have violated your "space." Your fear is that they might hit you, or that you might not be able to avoid hitting them, especially if the person in front of *them* makes a sudden change and thereby precipitates a chain reaction not-so-accidental accident. The secondary fear is that your car will be damaged with all the underlying issues that entails, or that you and your car's occupants may be injured or killed.

The event could be a death – a relationship, a pet, a person, or your own impending death. Many if not most people don't realize that the death of a relationship can be just as traumatic as an actual death. When a friend or loved one violates the perceived "rules of engagement" for the relationship, that relationship, at least in its current configuration, dies. So, for instance infidelity in an intimate relationship violates the rule of monogamy and the expectation of fidelity, and that aspect of the relationship dies. We'll talk more about the resulting process of grieving in Chapter 5.

The whole point is that something happens. I perceive that something has happened, and based on my perception I either like or dislike whatever it is that happened. If I like it, then I perceive it as positive. If I dislike it, I perceive it as negative, or bad. If the event is a significant enough disruption to my idea of how I want things to become, then I may have a tough time assimilating the new reality that does not conform to the way I wanted things to be. Forth springs the need to forgive.

Who... Or What

We tend to think of forgiving as being something related to another person. In other words the event is something that someone – a person – has done. But that's not the whole picture. There are any number of potential originators of an event, and not all of them are animate.

It may be another person – that's the usual suspect. Even though another person may be intelligent and even caring, they don't always do things the way I would want. Much as I would like, I cannot control other people. (Oops, did I almost slip into the Worldly mindset there of wanting to control?) I'm doing the best I can just to control myself, and I am not always successful at that. Naturally other people are going to do things I don't like or want whether deliberate or not, malicious or innocent. It just happens.

It may be an animal. While I might argue that animals are persons of a different sort, I understand that animals live in the moment and so it's not the same when something is done by an animal. There's not usually the same expectation of accountability with an animal. De-

The Energy of Forgiveness

pending on the relationship I have with the animal, the animal may fare better or worse in the aftermath of the event. A pet may get redirection or discipline. A spider or other multi-legged creature may get captured and put outside - at least that's what Ann and I do with them. A paper wasp… or a bear… may get the death sentence.

It may be an object. For example, how do you feel when you stub your toe on a piece of furniture? Do you want to smash it to bits, or push it out of a 20th story window – upon which it would be smashed to bits? I've broken a toe on a piece of furniture in the middle of the night when I got up in the dark to answer nature's call. My wife Ann regularly bashes her head on things like car door frames and other hard and relatively immovable objects. Sometimes when she does that I think she is as upset with her head for sticking out as she is at the doorframe or whatever object. Would her head be considered an inanimate object? I have mused aloud many times of getting her a protective helmet, like someone with a nervous disorder might wear. I assure you there's been many times I wished I'd been wearing one myself. My head is quite lumpy enough without extraneous help from inanimate objects.

It may be a natural event, what some might call an "act of God." For instance, it could be a rainstorm that forced a cancellation of a long-anticipated ball game, or lightening that forced a premature end to time at the swimming pool. I saw a video of lightening hitting a small river. The water nearly exploded out of the river's banks, and continued to churn for minutes afterwards. It could be an earthquake that damaged my home or other property. It could just be that the day is cloudy and misty when I wanted to do something outside. My son Jesse likes cloudy rainy weather, and so it's the sunshiny days that most people prefer that he doesn't like, because of his sometimes-faulty perception that the sunshine also makes things hot. We had a lot of hot, sunshiny days when we lived in Texas. The point here is that it may not be anything I can actually touch that caused the event. The question, the crux, is how I react to it. Do I accept it, or do I become upset or angry? Is my energy positive, neutral or negative?

Finally, it may be something that I myself have done – or not done – that becomes the event. When I stubbed my toe on the furniture, somewhere in the back of my mind I knew that I was the one who had neglected to be careful about where the furniture was, or to use some form of night-light so that I could see where I was going. It could be that I neglected to pay a bill, and now my credit score is impacted. Or I left something out in the yard that is now ruined due to the rain last night. It could be that I did – or neglected – something that damaged a relationship, either in malice or innocence. Often damage to a relationship is impossible or nearly impossible to repair. As we examined in the story of Judas, I am the one that I have the hardest time forgiving. The event keeps playing in my mind, again and again, each time I feel the remorse and regret, each time recognizing what it is that I could have done differently to produce a better outcome than the one I live with now. That can get to be pretty miserable.

The Energy of Forgiveness

Perceptions

We've talked about the need, the event, and the perpetrator – the cause of the event. But let's think about this. Events are happening all the time. All sorts of events are happening all the time, both natural events as well as those created by a person – human or otherwise – or circumstance. So what is it about some events that precipitate or create the need for forgiveness? It's really pretty simple: I don't like the event, or I don't like the outcome of the event.

The event in and of itself has no inherent value. It just is… what it is.

Let's take the broken vase for example. A vase falls off the table and smashes to bits. If I happen to like that vase, then I am upset that the vase is broken and effectively is no more. The more I like the vase, the more upset I am. If I am indifferent about the vase, I may be upset that there is now a mess to clean up, but the destruction of the vase itself is of no consequence. If I dislike the vase, I may actually feel good, or at least relieved, that it is now broken and gone.

There is a Japanese tradition called Kintsugi, of repairing pottery with gold, silver or platinum. Rather than trying to hide the cracks, attention is drawn to the repair through the ostentatious use of precious – and beautiful - metal. A piece of pottery that has been repaired in such a way is treasured all the more for its history. Some were even accused of deliberately smashing valuable pottery so that it could acquire the artful kintsugi gold seamed repair.

The point here is that the emotional content of the event is not tied to the event itself, or even really the object, but rather to *my perception of the event*. The emotions can run from a very negative upset-ness and grieving that it is broken to being glad that it's broken – because it's now gone – or being glad that it's broken because it is now art and even more cherished than before.

Death could be viewed the same way. If I hold an atheistic, existential viewpoint, then I may view death as being annihilation of the person. That could be very upsetting to say the least, especially if the person being annihilated is *me*. So my perception is that death is to be avoided at all costs - that death is the ultimate horrible event. Even for some religious people who believe in such a thing as hell and the concept that one must do something to avoid it, death is potentially even worse than annihilation.

On the other hand we will all die eventually. It's not the death that is important really because it is inevitable. It's the un-natural shortening of life that is the concern. But if life is uncertain, then who's to say that it's truly a shortening of the life but rather the natural end of life even if through unnatural means? My understanding of my life – my life as a spirit – is that it extends infinitely into the "past" and infinitely into the "future," at least from the point of view of my material perception of time. I've quoted "past" and "future" because space and time has no meaning in Spirit. If my life extends infinitely into the past and infinitely into the future, then the "time" involved in the mortal life that I am now experiencing is infinitely small, infinitely insignificant. Well, maybe not insignificant, but certainly not the hullabaloo we make it out to be. What applies to me also applies to everyone else as well – in terms of infinite life, any finite segment of mortal life is vanishingly small. And as such, in the eternal scheme of things, death is not really such a big thing.

My mother's passing is an example of this. She was diagnosed with Alzheimer's disease when she was 80 years old. The average life expectancy for an Alzheimer's is 8-10 years, and she was a few months shy of turning 89 when she passed. At first she simply had trouble remembering little details, like a word she wanted to use in a sentence, or someone's name. As time wore on, her memory became more and more sketchy, and her ability to think – her cognitive ability - also eroded. It was very much like she was aging backwards mentally. She certainly became more childlike later in the progression of the disease. It also seemed that her decline progressed in both a step-wise and exponential way. At first the decline was slow, but in the last two to three years there were relatively sudden, quite noticeable stair-step changes and those changes had increasing impact on her abilities. She became fragile in the sense that any significant change in her environment would degrade her condition as well. For instance, moving from her home of 50 years to an assisted living center resulted in a step down in cognitive ability. When that situation stopped working a relatively short time later, the next move also took a hit on her ability to think. Within the last year and a half or so of her life, she lost the ability to comprehend her condition. Beyond that point her life became more peaceful. She could only live in the "now" and enjoy the things she treasured such as her cat, her quilts, and, of course, meals except that Alzheimer's patients also lose their sense of taste. Finally she had an "event" which removed her ability to do anything for herself, and shortly after that she became unable to swallow and passed on within a week. A couple days before she actually passed, Ann had a vision of her, as a young woman, playing with her dog Chula who had passed two years before and was now romping around healthy and fit as well. We believe the vision was my mom's message that she had found release and that all was well with her now.

My point of this story is that for my mother, death was a good thing. She had lived a reasonably long and good life, and death for her represented a release from the challenges of a condition she found particularly distasteful. My mother, who had a master's degree in special education, who taught me to fly and earned her amateur radio operator's license, highly valued her intellect and abilities. Watching those abilities erode away must have been quite difficult and depressing for her. So death became her ticket to whatever the next big thing was to be for her. Even if I had believed in annihilation, I couldn't believe that keeping her in that state would be of benefit to her or anyone.

It's all in perception. An event is just an event. We make of it what we will based on our perception.

I am reminded of the Taoist story about an old farmer, which goes something like this:

There was an old farmer who had worked his crops for many years. One day his horse ran away. Upon hearing the news, his neighbors came to visit. "Such bad luck," they said sympathetically.

"Maybe," the farmer replied. The next morning the horse returned, bringing with it three wild mares. "How wonderful," the neighbors exclaimed.

"Maybe," replied the old man. The following day, his son tried to ride one of the untamed horses, was thrown, and broke his leg. The neighbors again came to offer their sympathy on his misfortune.

"Maybe," answered the farmer. The day after, military officials came to the village to draft young men into the army. Seeing that the son's leg was broken, they passed him by. The neighbors congratulated the farmer on how well things had turned out.

"Maybe," said the farmer.

The farmer perceived that events are just events. We may like or dislike the results of the event. Each event has the potential of being both a curse and a blessing. Our perception is what decides how we experience it.

Something Is Lost

We've talked about "the event" and the perception of the event. It's also important to examine what it is about the event and the perception of the event that fosters the negative emotions and energy tied to the event. I believe that it all boils down to a change, and along with the change the perception that something is lost.

In the case of the broken vase, the loss is of an object. There is also the loss of enjoyment of the object. As I pass through the room where the vase sits, and I see the vase, I remember all the details of the vase: how the vase came to be there, how beautiful I think it is, if it is a gift I remember the person who gave it to me and how I felt when I received it. All of these sights and memories are things I enjoy, things I like. There's a lot of *stuff* going on there. When the vase is destroyed, I may perceive that all the other things go with it. Certainly the vase as a reminder is gone. Things have changed, in a way I don't like.

If the result of the event is something that is physically painful, what is lost is, at least for a time, my ability to be comfortable, or my perception that the world is a safe and comfortable place to be. Pain, at least physical pain, is the natural mechanism our bodies use to encourage us to avoid whatever it is that caused the pain.

My standby example of the person in traffic who engages in unsafe behavior illustrates loss of safety. If I want to keep myself safe and free from pain or material loss, I will want to create an environment of safety. The other person's behavior may destroy my safe environment.

The Energy of Forgiveness

The Blame Game

I talked about the concept of shifting the blame to someone or something in Chapter 3 with the discussion of apology. The tendency, at least in the US, is to find someone to blame for the event, and place the blame as quickly as possible to deflect the possibility that the blame might land on them.

The important thing to note at this point is that there is the tendency to feel the need to blame. Yes, in some cases there is someone or something to blame. If I'm being careless and through my carelessness I cause injury, then certainly I am to blame.

I suppose I could also say that even if I was being careful, but something happened through my action that caused injury, I would still be to blame. In many cases however, there is no one to blame because "the event" is just something that happened. I could argue that if someone is being as careful as they can be, and their action causes injury, they are not truly to blame, because it's not truly their action that caused the injury. It was simply an accident. If I'm driving down the road at a safe speed and hit a patch of ice that I couldn't tell was there and as a result lose control of my vehicle and crash, am I really to blame? In the eyes of the law I am, because as the driver I am responsible for keeping my car under control at all times. But in practice it doesn't always happen that way. If my crash destroys the property of someone else – maybe the car I'm driving isn't mine, or I crashed into someone's car on the side of the road – that person may feel angry at me, even though functionally I am not to blame. It's simply an event; something that I could not anticipate or control.

Being able to blame some one or some thing gives me a focus for my negative emotions – my anger or whatever. It's harder to maintain negative emotions if I don't have a focal point for those emotions. That's not to say that I can't simply foster an attitude of anger in myself without having someone or something to direct the anger towards, but being able to affix the blame gives me a foundation to build on with those negative emotions.

Check out http://theenergyofforgiveness.com/chapter-4 for additional material.

Chapter 5
The Process Of Grieving

"Grief can be the garden of compassion. If you keep your heart open through everything, your pain can become your greatest ally in your life's search for love and wisdom."
— Rumi

The Five Stages of Grieving

It's important at this point to examine the process of grieving as separate from the process of forgiving. I discussed in Chapter 4 the concept that something is lost relative to the event that generates a need for forgiveness. Anytime there is loss, there is a process of grieving that takes place. This is natural – it is the process of emotionally processing the loss. This process includes recognizing that things are not as they were, letting go of *what was*, and embracing, or at least accepting, the *what is*. This is what makes grieving healthy whereas non-forgiveness is not, because grieving is a natural process of assimilating change.

There is a well-understood process that people go through when they grieve. We normally think of grieving as something that happens when a loved one passes, but in reality, and as mentioned previously, this process is triggered anytime there is a loss. There are distinct stages to this process as we'll discuss in this chapter. The stages don't necessarily linearly define the process – as I grieve I may skip some stages or skip back and forth between stages. This is all normal. I may get stuck in one stage – this is not normal, at least not long-term.

Understanding this process can be very helpful in processing the grief. When my brother Mike passed, my psychiatrist father, who was mightily suffering through his grief process at the time, taught me about the process. Because I intellectually understood the process, I could metaphorically stand outside of myself and recognize the emotions as I experienced them, and know that this is a normal part of the process and that I was not "going off the deep end" so to speak. I felt reassured in the process and it enabled me to experience the process in a more-or-less healthy way.

Later on in life when I experienced the death of a relationship, I learned how the grieving process was triggered by that type of event as well rather than just by a physical death. Even if the death of relationship is intentional, meaning that I've found the relationship to be toxic enough that I deliberately ended the relationship, the grieving process is still there. This is part of what happens in messy divorces – one or both of the couple get somewhat "stuck" in the anger stage.

Finally, I learned on my own that grieving also applies to objects as well, such as when a favorite vase is broken. You might say the grieving process is triggered by the death of the relationship with the object. The grieving process could be triggered by the loss of a body part. I would expect that someone who has lost a limb or even lost the function of a limb through stroke, injury or disease, would find themselves processing through the stages of grief.

Denial

The first stage of grieving is denial. This is especially noticeable when the death is sudden, such as in an accident. I'm sure you remember instances of someone screaming "NO!" when something awful has happened.

I learned about my brother's passing by receiving a message that I had a call from a sister. When I called her back, she was almost incredulous that I didn't know what had happened, and then she told me through her tears "Mike died." There really wasn't much for me to say or even think at that point, I felt numb. I remember telling my boss what had happened. Our conversation was a bit disjointed. He said he was sorry to hear that. I said I didn't know what I was going to do next. He said that was all he could do – say he was sorry. I always thought that was an odd response, but I recognize in retrospect that he was just acknowledging his helplessness to do anything that would be of use to me. I tried to continue working through the fog that day, but as the reality – or seeming unreality – of the event sunk in, I recognized that I needed to go home to take care of myself emotionally.

Even years after Mike's passing, I had the feeling that he wasn't really gone, that at any moment I would get news that there was a big mistake, that he hadn't really died but had for some reason been unable to come forward. I even dreamed once that his body was still alive, and someone else was inhabiting it. That was a bizarre dream, but it was interesting that in the dream I still felt the need for connection even though I knew it wasn't really my brother.

The experience may be a bit different for the death of relationship. The denial may take the form of continuing the charade of the relationship for the sake of appearances, or becoming fixated on the partner who has gone, expecting them to return at any time, or even just denying that anything is wrong.

Anger

A common expression of the anger stage is being angry with someone who has passed. The bereaved person may even think "how could you do this to me?" A particular challenge with this gut reaction is that the follow-on is a feeling of guilt for being angry at someone for their own death. It just adds to the bundle of mixed-up emotions to deal with in the situation, but the reaction is real and maybe unavoidable. A healthy dose of self-forgiveness is in order here don't you think?

My brother died in a helicopter accident. As the details came out later it became clear that his death was the result of incompetence and carelessness on the part of the pilot and copilot.

Allow me to digress for a moment. The reason the helicopter my brother was riding in crashed was because the person at the controls, the co-pilot, decided his instruments were incorrect, and used his own judgment to gauge his altitude above the water. The reason his judgment and the instruments disagreed is because they were flying at night over water – the Gulf of Mex-

The Energy of Forgiveness

ico – under an overcast sky. The only thing they could see was the drilling rig they were approaching. They couldn't see stars above, nor the waters below. These are by definition what is called in the world of aviation "instrument conditions" or "IFR," which stands for Instrument Flight Rules, meaning that you need the skills to fly by instruments alone to fly in these conditions, practically if not legally. In the Bahamas, night flying is legally IFR but in the U.S. it is not. Under these conditions, it is impossible to judge altitude, or just about any other attitude be it right-side-up or up-side-down. Why did the co-pilot not understand this? *Because he did not have the instrument flying skillset – he was not instrument rated.* As an instrument-rated pilot myself, I understand the folly of his action. But because he wasn't instrument rated, he didn't know any better. Because he was not instrument rated, the person who was practically, if not legally, responsible was the pilot. Apparently the pilot wasn't paying attention to what was going on, and only "woke up" to the situation a few seconds before they hit the water – at 1000 feet per minute descent. That's 16 feet per second – a pretty good clip. Five hundred feet per minute is considered a normal IFR approach descent rate.

What was the co-pilot's mistake? When faced with a problem, he failed to ask for help or advice from the real pilot-in-command. So what was the pilot's mistake? Allowing a non-instrumented-rated co-pilot to fly the helicopter under his command under effective IFR conditions without himself keeping a watchful eye on what was going on.

Paul McKinley

After the helicopter crashed, it ended up-side-down in the water, with the flotation device holding the door shut. The pilot and co-pilot managed to get out and climbed on top of the helicopter. The one passenger that survived couldn't open the door, so – underwater – he put his back against a window and his feet against a bulkhead and pushed the window out of its frame. When he reached the surface of the water, the pilot and co-pilot were telling each other "if they aren't out by now they aren't coming out." The one passenger went back under the fuel-contaminated water and tried to reach inside the cabin to rescue other passengers, but couldn't. At least he tried, even if the two responsible did not.

So for me there was definitely a focal point for anger – the pilot and co-pilot. And there were any number of different aspects that I could be angry about.

Do you recognize the blame game starting up here? You might say that affixing blame in this case is appropriate, but please hold on to the distinction that blame – or responsibility - is separate from the event itself.

I've also experienced the anger phase while grieving the death of a relationship. I found myself being angry for what seemed to me to be no good reason. I even sought help from a psychologist, who introduced me to the M. Scott Peck MD book "The Road Less Travelled" and by association Dr. Peck's other books, especially "Further Along The Road Less Travelled" where I learned about stages of spiritual growth which I described in my book "Rules of the Spirit."

The Energy of Forgiveness

Bargaining

The typical example of bargaining is the pleading prayer with God to make the situation different, to make it not so. Usually this comes in the form of "I'll do this if you'll fix this." For example, "God if you'll fix this for me I'll go to church every Sunday for the rest of my life," as if going to church was to God's benefit.

Another form of bargaining might be offering or agreeing to do things to salvage a dying relationship. Please understand that there are many times when a partner needs to adjust behavior for the sake of the relationship, and this is a normal part of the give and take of relationships. Where this becomes dysfunctional is in one-sided or abusive relationships. I would say that bargaining to "try harder" or whatever other concession in a relationship where the other person is being abusive or has effectively already "checked out" is going down the path of co-dependency. Frankly, there are some relationships that I believe are not salvageable, or are not worth the effort even if they were salvageable. This type of relationship needs to be allowed to die a peaceful death. No amount of bargaining or changing behavior is going to really do any good. The likelihood is that even if short-term change is effected, eventually the person's habits will reassert themselves and the unhealthy cycle will begin again.

Bargaining is, in a way, just another form of denial. There is a tiny bit of acceptance, in that at least there is recognition that something unwanted has happened or is happening, but there's an underlying of denial that what is, *is*. There's still a holding on to *what was*, a resistance to the change that has happened or is in process.

Depression

Depression is really the first step in acceptance. When I reach the point of depression, I have recognized that things are not as they were, and never will be again. Whatever was, is no longer; it is gone. I'm still quite emotionally attached to the way things were, so I am naturally unhappy to have lost whomever or whatever (there's that "something lost" part), so I feel bad – I feel depressed about that loss.

Even though depression may seem to be the bottom of the valley, it seems to me that it is really the top of the hill so to speak. The stages leading up to depression are composed of holding on to what was, to fighting the situation and trying to recreate or patch up the old status, to dragging my feet in order to resist the change. When I reach depression, I am no longer resisting the change. I have worn myself out resisting the change and I can no longer keep up the exercise in futility of resisting the change. Depression is the emotion of "giving up." Even though it is rooted in the past, depression is the "dying within" of the *what was*.

The dying, though, clears the way for what is *becoming*, for what is *new*, for what is *now*.

Acceptance

If depression is the "top of the hill," then acceptance is the trip down the other side. That's not to say that it's easy, just that the hard work has been done. Rather than battling to hang on to the *what was* that can no longer be, I have begun to adapt, to find new ways of forward, to learn new behaviors, to like new things. I have begun to truly embrace the change and build a new life map of how things will be for me going forward.

Per the description found in grief.com, acceptance should not be confused with being okay with what has happened. While in some cases this might be the case, this is not what acceptance is all about. Certainly I am not okay and never will be with what happened to my brother. Acceptance is simply the act of moving forward through having let go of the *what was* – of spending effort and positivity in the new, post-traumatic-event world. Acceptance is the positive form of living in the *now*. Acceptance is the healthy continuance of the evolution of *who I am*.

The Connection: Grieving and Forgiveness

There's a point to this discussion of grieving relative to forgiveness. Grieving is a normal, healthy process, a process of adapting to significant change. Change happens. Staying healthy both emotionally, physically, and spiritually means adapting, and grieving is just that: adapting to the upset of change. I'm sure you'll agree: grieving isn't much fun. It's emotionally painful. But so is running a race. The exercise is healthy. The process is healthy. Your muscles and maybe other body parts complain a lot. It's important to recognize that, at least until a degree of spiritual growth is attained, change will be painful. Grieving is the process of letting go of that pain.

The difference between grieving and unforgiveness is that unforgiveness is essentially the act of getting stuck in the grieving process. Rather than letting go of the *what was*, unforgiveness hangs on to the pain and the negative emotions tied to the event. If you have a boil, eventually the boil will erupt and the putrified material will drain away and the body will heal itself. It's painful, but the pain goes away as the boil heals. That is the process of grieving. Unforgiveness is the careful preservation of the putrification, holding it in so that the body cannot heal, and potentially having the boil grow as well as other areas also become infected. The longer this goes on, the worse things become.

It's important to understand that it is natural to experience negative emotions as a result of an upsetting event. I believe that it is possible to spiritually outgrow this – to learn to recognize in the moment, *in the now*, all of the things that have been described, and as such assimilate natural changes in such a way that the pain is experienced in a way that, if you'll pardon my way of looking at it, isn't painful. It's not a question of being stoic about it. It's not about feeling the pain without expressing it. It's an accepting of things that are best accepted and looking beyond them to the *what is becoming*. It's not an avoiding or ignoring the pain, but rather transcending it.

Remember to check http://theenergyofforgiveness.com/chapter-5 for additional material.

Chapter 6
What It Means To Forgive

"It's one of the greatest gifts you can give yourself, to forgive."
– Maya Angelou

Letting Go

Let's examine forgiveness itself. What does it mean to forgive? In its most basic sense forgiving means letting go of the negative emotions, the negative "energy" associated with an event. Is it easy? Well, at first maybe not. Although I think that as you grow spiritually and exercise that "forgive" muscle, it becomes easier in time.

I discussed the Law of Attraction in "Rules of the Spirit." My paraphrase of the Law of Attraction is "Whatever I put energy into gets bigger," meaning that whatever I think about, talk about, watch or act on will increase. I "resonate" with whatever I focus upon, and things or events that resonate with my focus are attracted to me. As people become more adept with the Law of Attraction, they become more aware of where their emotions and their energy are going, and they learn to let the negative emotions go faster and without as much drama. That's because they understand that the negative energy is going to manifest more negative experiences into their lives.

I discussed in Chapter 4 the concept that forgiveness is associated with an event. It's actually not the event itself, but rather your *perception* of the event. The need to forgive is triggered by negative emotion, and the negative emotion is triggered by an event, but it's really our *perception* of the event, that the event is "bad," that results in the negative emotion. But this is a judgment, and we have control over our judgment. Events in and of themselves are not good or bad. It's really more a question of whether you like or dislike whatever it is – whether you enjoy it or not.

Just as an example, you might say that pain is bad. Okay, I understand that you may not enjoy pain. However, pain can be associated with things that you might judge to be good, such as the pain that results from exercise that you're not used to doing. As avid exercise people say: "No pain, no gain." I've already used lancing a boil as an example. It's not much fun during the process, but the alternative is a maybe lower grade but much longer term pain, or even a boil that continues to get worse. So yes, you may not enjoy it much at the time, but your perception of the event is that it is "good." Would you feel unforgiving towards someone who had lanced a painful boil for you so that it could begin to heal? I would think gratefulness would be more in order. I'm reminded of the song by the musical group Chicago "If She Would Have Been Faithful." The song tells the story of a person who realizes that the "wrong" a past partner did resulted in something much better in their life. Even though there was betrayal and death of a relationship, which triggered a voyage through the painful process of grieving, the lyrics express gratefulness: "I want to thank her (thank her again)."

The challenge in forgiving is the perception of "bad"-ness in the moment. It's hard to let go of that. The fact is that forgiving is a *conscious* decision, a deliberate act, at least at first until it becomes habit. And of course the more energy you put into the event and the negative emotion, the more the event and emotion gets bigger, so sometimes it takes re-deciding, and re-deciding, and re-deciding. And re-deciding. That's part of what Jesus was referring to with the "seventy times seven" or "whatever it takes" remark: you just have to keep at it, to keep deciding to let the negative emotions go, until there's no longer any negative emotion associated with the event. You just have to *keep deciding* it's not worth it; it's not hurting anyone besides yourself, and let it go. Again.

Finally, it helps to understand that all things and all events are good. "Count it all Joy, my brothers, when you meet trials of various kinds, for you know that the testing of your faith produces steadfastness" (James 1:2-3 ESV). When you begin to perceive all things as good, even when you don't enjoy it much in the moment, it changes the whole character of your perception of things and events around you. I would go as far as to say you may get to the point where you no longer feel the need to forgive because you no longer feel the negative emotions related to events that aren't very enjoyable. You <u>can</u> get to the point where your focus is on the mystical anticipation of the good you know will result, without knowing what it will be in the moment. The negative emotion just doesn't come up. It isn't there. There's nothing to forgive! It's not that you're refusing to forgive, or in denial about your need to forgive. It's just that the negative energy never entered the picture. Forgiveness is about letting go of negative emotions; negative, destructive energy.

Forgive & Forget – the Misconception

Now, don't get me wrong on forgiveness. A common phrase is "forgive and forget." There are two basic problems with this concept. One is that forgetting prevents me from setting and enforcing healthy boundaries. If I simply forget, I am none the wiser and would likely allow the same violation again and again. This is not healthy! The other is that it denies who I am, because a part of who I am and the experience, knowledge and skills that I have are the result of my experiences *both good and "bad."* I do not support the concept of forgetting the incident, but rather that the forgiver would do best to totally and completely release any negative emotional content attached to the event.

Let's look at the violation of boundary problem first. Let's say I have a friend who frequently calls me in the middle of the night just to chat. Now maybe I like to chat with this person so it isn't a problem. On the other hand, if it is disrupting my sleep and I am beginning to suffer from that, I need to set boundaries. I need to ask this person to call during a time when I'm normally awake – and let them know I need to be left alone during certain hours. If I then promptly forget the situation, and they continue to call during my sleep time, I have not been successful in asserting and maintaining my boundaries. If forgiveness means forgetting, then the situation is likely to continue, and I am the one that will suffer. My boundaries will be violated again and again. Effectively I have no boundaries, and that doesn't seem very healthy to me. I must be able to remember what has happened in order to maintain my boundaries – in order to arrange my life so that my needs are met.

The other problem is that the event itself is part of your experience: it's part of who you at this point. There are gifts to be had, lessons to be learned, spiritual growth to be gained in any and every incident, regardless of whether we enjoy them at the time or not. Honor your experience! Honor your life! Really forgetting an incident would mean you miss out on the hard-earned gifts, the blessings that result from less-than-enjoyable experiences. It would also mean failing to learn from the incident. Often I learn things for myself by observing the "mistakes" others make. I'd much rather learn by others' mistakes than having to experience it for myself! But even more so I want to learn by my own mistakes – after all, I paid for the knowledge with the pain of the experience! Tying forgetfulness with forgiveness would interfere with that learning. It's just too valuable to forget.

Tying forgetfulness with forgiveness also presents an impossible task. It is impossible for a healthy person to truly forget anything. Hypnotists have proven that even small details can be dredged from someone's memory through the use of hypnosis. And even without that, you can find yourself being reminded of things long forgotten by something that happens or something you see in the moment. Do you remember things you've done that you wish you hadn't done? If you didn't remember those things, you might be condemned to reliving them. If you do them often enough, other people will start remembering them for you. Instead of building a good reputation, you'd be building a negative one!

There's also the concept of being careful what you pray for. My mother was a strong believer in just forgetting things she didn't want to remember. If there was anything she didn't like, or didn't want to think about, she just decided that she would forget about it. Her solution to things she didn't like was to forget. I mentioned earlier that she eventually developed Alzheimer's or similar dementia, which started out with simply not being *able* to remember things. Do the two go together? Did the insistence on forgetting actively result in the dementia? No one will ever know for sure, but I have noticed that diseases are often symbolic of the way we live and think. Ann and I have been aware of the symbolic relationship between emotions and diseases. I knew of one person whom I had identified as being, as I called it, "shaking in his boots" from constant fear. Nobody else really identified him as being fearful, but it was obvious to me. This person ended up developing and dying from brain cancer. We looked up brain cancer and as you may have guessed, the underlying emotion was fear.

There is biblical reference to God forgetting our sins in Isaiah 43:25: "Remember your sins no more." However, there is another verse earlier in Isaiah 1:18 that says "Though your sins are like scarlet, they shall be white as snow." The point here is that it is *not* that the "sin" itself

The Energy of Forgiveness

is forgotten, just that it is not remembered *as* sin. The negativity associated with it is resolved and dissolved. I believe God simply doesn't remember them as transgressions but rather as situations we put ourselves in or through, which become opportunities to grow. I can almost hear God having a good laugh about the "sins" I've committed.

I discussed "sin" in Chapter 9 of *The Rules of the Spirit*. The word "sin" is commonly understood in western Christian religious circles as meaning "breaking God's law" or to put it in a more typical and abrasive mindset "crimes against God," as if God were vulnerable to human crimes. The concept of a "sin against God" seems a bit narcissistic to me, like making mankind more powerful than poor helpless God. The word "sin" in Spanish simply means "without," "absent," or "missing." So to me "sin" basically means something that puts distance or separation between myself and God – something that interferes with or reduces the connection - as if it was really possible to do such a thing. It doesn't hurt God, but it does create challenges in my human experience. Is it bad? Well, that depends on the perception. Personally I believe God gets the equivalent of a good belly laugh out of the whole concept, kind of like watching a kitten chase its tail.

The Higher Good would be better served by coming to recognize the blessings that have resulted from the event and learning to be thankful for the blessings. This won't necessarily happen overnight. Many times it's taken me years to recognize the blessings that have come from an event. My current philosophy is to recognize that the blessings are there – and be thankful for them - even though they may not be immediately obvious. Isn't that the "seventy times seven" perfection of releasing the negative emotion: to become thankful for the blessings brought by the event?

There's more material at http://theenergyofforgiveness.com/chapter-6 - check it out!

Chapter 7
The Energy Of Forgiveness

"To forgive is to set a prisoner free and discover that the prisoner was you."
— Louis B. Smedes

Fruits of the Spirit

I've mentioned earlier my understanding of spiritual life as continuing from the infinite past into the infinite future, with the possibility of an occasional sashay into the material existence. Let's dig into that a bit deeper. Part of what that implies is that when a baby is born, the person or "soul" inside that infant body is not newly created, but rather Spirit. When I was born, I didn't just suddenly (or in the course of 9-1/2 months) spring into being. I was and am Spirit – that spark of energy that cannot be measured. The part of me that makes me *me* already existed even before conception.

So what does it mean to be born out of Spirit world into the physical world?

One of Ann's insights is that we are born into the world with what she calls the "Fruits of the Spirit." When we are born into the world, we have no concept of the Rules of the World. We are born with love. Have you ever seen a baby that hated his or her parents, or anyone else? We are born with grace. We are born with Trust. Have you ever seen a newborn that did not trust those who are taking care of her/him? If a newborn baby always started crying when a certain person came in the room, wouldn't you wonder what was going on there?

The point here is that newborns are fresh from Spirit; they understand life from a spiritual perspective. They haven't yet been taught the Rules of the World. So there are no barriers to healthy energy flow, or "chi." There's no concept of scarcity. They are fresh from Heaven you might say, and experience life in that way.

As a child begins to be immersed in the world, they begin to learn the Rules of the World. They are taught scarcity. They are taught mistrust. The child is taught fear by those who would use fear to get the child to do what they want. They are taught attachment to things or people.

When I form attachments to things, places, or people, there is an energy connection to that whatever-it-is. I am investing my psychic energy into it. One of the things I've learned is that the more "stuff" I have, the more energy it takes from me. And I have a lot of "stuff!"

My mentor Raymond Aaron and his wife Karyn share a philosophy of maintaining a "sparse" life. Even though he is quite wealthy, he has few material possessions, because he understands that the possessions can drain his energy. Instead of having lots of clutter, he has a few really nice things that make his life easier and better rather than being just more stuff. Each possession is chosen to provide an everyday benefit or enjoyment.

The Energy of Forgiveness

The challenge comes in when something that I've become attached to changes or goes away. My energy field is disrupted; my energy pathways become blocked. Imagine a garden hose that has water flowing through it. When I step on the hose, either purposefully or accidentally, the water flow is restricted. I might hear sound coming from the hose – the engineer in me knows that sound comes from cavitation. If the pressure is higher than the strength of the hose, the hose may start to bulge and become damaged as a result of the restriction of flow. If, instead of water, the hose was carrying oxygen for me to breathe, it probably wouldn't take long before I began to suffer from suffocation.

Our energy, or "chi" pathways are like that. They can become restricted, and the restriction is harmful.

EFT: the roto-rooter of energy pathways.

I mentioned EFT in Chapter 6 of *The Rules of the Spirit*. EFT is a powerful tool for letting go of negative emotions. I'll explain EFT here by providing a story from my experience.

Shortly after the birth of our son Jesse, Ann began to experience panic attacks. A panic attack is basically fear that has gone what engineers call "open loop" meaning there is nothing to keep it from almost instantly increasing to the point of being debilitating or even causing unconsciousness. Ann's first panic attack was brought on by being in a church classroom full of people, listening to someone teach about panic attacks. Beginning to feel claustrophobic, she went out to "get some air" and then found herself laying on the ground looking up at one of the physicians in the congregation who had come to look after her.

The panic attack experience was pretty debilitating for her. Since she was staying at home with our son, she was responsible for his care, as well as getting the groceries and other shopping that was necessary. But going into the grocery store, or especially the large discount stores, was a trigger for the panic attack. The fact that she had our son with her, and the knowledge that if she became incapacitated he would be at risk, only served to make things worse. Panic attacks being unrestrained fear, anything that adds fear increases the risk and severity of the panic attack.

Fortunately a friend who is an energy worker recommended someone to Ann who used an acupressure process called NAET (Nabudripad's Allergy Elimination Technique) to treat allergies. I know this doesn't seem to have anything to do with panic attacks, but please bear with me. Ann had been experiencing worse and worse allergy symptoms as well during this time, to the point that nine months out of the year she could hardly breathe, and was having asthma attacks to go along with the panic attacks – what a combination! Ann kept telling herself: "If the allergies can get worse and worse, why can't they get better and better?" So, even though the idea of using acupressure – tapping – to eliminate allergies "weirded her out" she went and was treated for lactose intolerance. Mind you, Ann's lactose intolerance was so bad that just a tablespoon of milk would have her in the bathroom in agony for hours. Her very first treatment eliminated her lactose intolerance! She still had a bit of gas from cheese, but the practitioner said that cheese had "fallen out" so he retreated her for the cheese on the next visit, and since then she's been able to eat or drink milk products with impugnity, including and maybe most especially ice cream!

We were so impressed that Ann kept going back to get *all* her allergies removed. Her attitude was "I want 'em ALL gone!" She continued with about 6 months of going back every two weeks or so, with different allergies being treated each time. When she was finally treated for grasses, the asthma went away. She'd had occasional eczema as well before treatment, which went away as well; that was an unexpected bonus. I'll address NAET further in this chapter, but meantime Ann was so impressed with the results of the NAET that she became intrigued with energy medicine techniques/modalities. She started reading up on it, and through that research came across EFT – Emotional Freedom Technique. She recognized that EFT could be her ticket out of panic attacks, so she learned everything she could about EFT and practiced it on herself... and resolved her panic attacks!

So, if EFT can resolve such a powerful debility as panic attacks, what is it? From a practical, functional perspective, it is merely a stimulation of the bodies' energy pathways through tapping. When Ann first started learning about it, the technique involved a lot of steps such as moving the eyes, singing "happy birthday" and other things that were pretty complicated. But as time went on, the main evangelist for EFT, Gary Craig, learned to condense it into a fairly simple process of tapping seven points (five on the face, one between the collar bones, and one under the arm) and verbal affirmations that were just as effective as the complicated rigamarole.

Ann was so impressed with the EFT, and it was so effective at resolving her debilitating panic attacks, that she became an EFT practitioner for a time. She is really good at it, too. She is able to use her psychic intuition to tune in to the emotional issues of the person she's working with, so that she's able to choose or create phrases that quickly get to the crux of the recipient's emotional issue.

We don't know exactly how EFT works. The best understanding that we have, and I'm loosely quoting Gary Craig, is that *all negative emotions are caused by a blockage in the energy pathways.* By stimulating the meridian pressure points through tapping while directing the thoughts and attention, the blockages can be removed. Once the blockage is removed, the negative emotion simply ceases to exist.

Many, if not most, of our aches and pains are emotionally based and therefore subject to elimination through EFT. One day Ann and I went to an instrument shop to have the altimeter for our airplane calibrated. There was a gentleman working in the shop who was bent over, and the expression on his face clearly showed that he was having a lot of back pain. I approached him and said "You seem to be in a lot of pain. Do you want to get rid of that? My wife here can take care of it for you." You know what went through his mind at that point – that she was going to do something to "pop" his back, which was going to hurt. He winced and shied away. She told him "I'm not going to hurt you, I'm not even going to touch you. It's just light tapping, and I'll show you how to do it." With that assurance, he agreed to let her work with him. After about 5-10 minutes, three or so "rounds," check how he's doing, and then another three or so "rounds," his pain was gone. He was standing erect and his face was relaxed. Even the other people in the shop were amazed, and asked "what did you do to him?" In discussing what happened, it came out that his wife had an asthma attack the night before, and he'd felt helpless to assist her, so his back had "enabled" his helplessness. Through resolving the feeling of helplessness, the pain was resolved.

Natural flow of energy: Meridians

Since we've referred to the energy pathways a bit here, let's go back and talk about them specifically. I'll give a bit of an explanation here, but if you're not familiar with energy meridians I recommend doing an Internet search and read up on the topic. It's quite fascinating.

Basically energy meridians, often referred to as just "meridians," are pathways in the body that channel the flow of spirit energy through the body. This is well known in Asian (China, Japan, Tibet, India, and other countries) medical culture, but has only recently become somewhat known in western culture. Even now it is often not well received by western medicine culture, despite the fact that it is proven to work so well. It's not accepted because it is not based on recognized "science." The spirit energy, "qi" or "chi" as the Chinese call it or "ki" as the Japanese call it, is not something you can measure with current scientific instruments. I suspect mankind will never be able to build a mechanical or electronic device that will truly be able to measure chi because chi is a totally different substance than matter or electricity. You can find diagrams online that show the meridians in the body. Remember though, they are not structural in the physical sense. You can't point to an energy meridian like you can a blood vessel or lymph node.

To quote natural-health-zone.com, "Energy blockages can be the result of stress, an injury or trauma, or bad living habits (diet, habits/addictions, lack of exercise) and can be traced to the root of all health (physical/mental/spiritual) problems. Our energy flow affects how we feel, how we think, and the over all condition of our health situation. When the body's life-force energy becomes blocked, various imbalances will result." The imbalances result in dis-ease, pain, and emotional discomfort.

So when you go to an acupuncturist, what they are doing is tapping into those energy pathways, and helping to reduce or eliminate the blockages so that the chi energy can flow and the body can become more vital.

NAET – allergies as an emotional response to elements in the environment

I mentioned NAET as being Ann's introduction to what's becoming known as "energy medicine." Energy medicine covers many concepts, practices, and modalities including acupuncture, acupressure, healing methods such as Quantum Touch, Bodytalk, Reiki, and many others. I personally believe that some or several

The Energy of Forgiveness

forms of energy medicine were used by Jesus of Nazareth to do his healings. I am a Reiki level 2 practitioner, although I only learned of Reiki as a result of Ann telling a fellow conference participant what I was doing on my own, and they told her "that sounds like Reiki." Even chiropractors work with energy medicine, although they tend to be focused on the nervous system, which is different than the meridian system. You may have heard of "chakras," which are part of the meridian system.

An interesting aspect of energy medicine from the perspective of someone who is focused on spiritual growth is that because it deals with spirit energy it can't be measured – only the results can be measured. And although we can begin to understand some aspects of it, and generally feel as if we understand and can explain what's going on, we don't and probably never will fully understand it. But I don't need to fully understand something to make use of it, just as I don't need to understand anything about electricity to use a light switch. I discover through practice that when I flip this little lever up, the lights come on, and when I flip it down, the lights go off. So, if I want the room to be lit I flip the lever up, and I get light.

NAET was originally developed as an acupuncture technique, but has been adapted to be performed by acupressure – tapping. You can read more about it online, especially at naet.com where you can also find a practitioner near you. During a NAET treatment, the practitioner uses muscle testing to discover substances that trigger the person's allergies. The practitioner then has the person hold a vial with that substance "in their energy field" - in their hand next to their chest above the heart

- and performs a series of tapping along the spine, and sometimes stimulation of other pressure points such as between the toes and/or beween the thumb and forefinger through massage. Some practitioners use a manual device to do the tapping while others use an electric vibrating "tapper." The person is then allowed to relax for a few minutes – with the allergen still held in their energy field. When the treatment is done, the person merely avoids the allergen for 25 hours, and they're done! The NAET protocol includes some allergens that must be treated before others, so sometimes several things will need to be treated before getting to the allergen that is causing the more noticeable problem That's why Ann kept going back every two weeks. They'd work on the "do first" allergens, and then figure out what was left. It's possible that her asthma was caused by other allergens as well as the grasses, but it was when she was treated for the grasses that she noticed the change. She said it was like little bubbles popping in her sinuses after the treatment, after which her sinuses drained and her asthma was gone.

The concept behind NAET is that the body's energy field senses the presence of the allergen and reacts to it. The reaction is a defensive mechanism. Through the treatment, the body's defense mechanism is "reset" with respect to that allergen. It is trained to recognize that the allergen is not a threat and is okay to have in its energy field.

Ann and I have come to recognize that, generally speaking, allergies are caused by an emotional trauma that was somehow associated with the substance. For instance, if I was eating ice cream when I learned that a loved one was injured, I might develop an allergy to ice cream. Usually we don't remember the event that formed the basis of the allergy, but it's still there.

I mentioned previously that EFT resolves emotional trauma. You might guess that it could also be used to eliminate allergies, and you'd be correct! Although, NAET seems to be more effective and reliable.

My Experiences with NAET

I mentioned Ann's experience with NAET, especially with regard to the lactose intolerance. We've had great fun over the years since then telling friends who suffer from lactose intolerance about NAET. When they go get treated for it, we throw an ice-cream party for them to celebrate!

I personally have had a number of treatments that have improved my quality of life. I used to have fairly significant allergies to some forms of fungus and house dust. There's a particular fungus that grows in the woods called a "devil's snuffbox" that was a strong allergen for me. It looks a bit like a dirty marshmallow, and it puts out a puff of brown dust – spores – when it's stepped on. If I stepped on one, I would have a severe allergic reaction 3-4 hours later. It would start with a stomachache and progress to hives, swelling of fingers, lips and nose. It could be a bit scary! House dust from sweeping up could give me hives.

At one point I developed an allergy to jalapeño peppers. I didn't realize what it was at first. One day I went to a Mexican restaurant with a friend, and four hours later I was sick and vomiting. I just chalked it up to bad food from the restaurant. But then later I had another similar reaction after eating jalapeños, and I realized it was a food allergy. So, I went and was treated for it. Now I can eat them without fear. In fact I use them as a preventative for colds and flu. I say "a jalapeño a day keeps the doctor away!" It works especially well if I visualize the capsaicin killing all the bugs in my throat as it goes down.

I've not had any hives or "toss my cookies" allergy experiences since being treated for jalapeños.

Unforgiveness – creating restriction

You may have been wondering what all this business about EFT and NAET has to do with the subject of this book: forgiveness. But this book is not just about forgiveness. It's about the _energy_ of forgiveness! This section is where the rubber hits the road: where we really start to focus on the *energetic* aspects of forgiveness. But this section is just the start – it's the segue into the deeper discussion. It's what you need to understand to stay with me as I dive deeper in the next few chapters. Hang on!

By now, you have a smattering of understanding of chi, or spirit energy. I've talked about the emotional connection with chi, or is it chi's connection with emotions. I've talked about the emotional connection with pain – both emotional and physical pain - as a result of the disturbance or restriction of chi. I've talked about the relationship between allergies and chi. I've talked about how forgiveness is related to an event and more specifically the perception of an event, which leads to an *emotional* response to the event. Are you getting the picture of how these things are all related?

What is really happening when I am unforgiving is that I am holding on to what was. I am resisting the tide of change, when change is inevitable. Remember the analogy of the garden hose? If the flow through the garden hose is the tide of change, then restricting that flow is bound to cause problems. Unforgiveness causes a restriction of the flow of chi in the body. Or maybe I should say that unforgiveness *is* a restriction of the flow of chi in the body. Unforgiveness is a restriction of chi, which is *spirit* energy, in the body.

I mentioned in *The Rules of the Spirit* that I rejected the idea that spiritual growth had to be accompanied by pain, and Ann's insight that the pain was not caused by the spiritual growth, but rather the resistance to the growth – the hanging on to what *was* rather than embracing what *is becoming*. So if it is the resisting that causes pain, then it would seem to follow that the emotional pain of the "event" resulting in a need for forgiveness is the result of resisting the change that the event brings about. Maybe even the physical pain in some circumstances is the result of resisting the change.

Resisting the change causes a disturbance or restriction of chi, which causes pain, and other undesirable outcomes that we'll explore in the next chapter.

Keep up the learning at http://theenergyofforgiveness.com/chapter-7 .

Chapter 8
The Emotional Origins
Of Dis-Ease

"Part of being a healthy person is being well integrated and at peace."
— Candace Pert

Dis-ease: a non-natural state

Now we start talking about dis-ease. I hyphenate the word as many spiritual writers and healers do, to emphasize that dis-ease is a lack of ease. From a spiritual perspective we are not born into dis-ease. Our bodies are wonderfully crafted to be self-sustaining. Researchers say that our bodies replace themselves with a mostly new set of cells every seven to ten years. Some of the most important parts are replaced even more frequently – apparently colon cells only last a few days. We have a wonderful multi-layered immune system that collaborates with some micro-organisms while it defends against others. We have a heart that pumps blood through our bodies without us even thinking about it: it just works automatically. There's a lot to it. But dis-ease isn't part of the plan. It isn't normal. Dis-ease represents that something is wrong.

Paul McKinley

In Western society we are used to thinking about dis-ease as being caused by some form of pathogen, or by genetics. To a degree, that's true. But let's look at an example. Let's say I'm driving down the highway, but I become distracted by something. Because I'm distracted, I don't notice the car is wandering towards the edge of the pavement. There's a bit of unevenness at the edge of the pavement where the top layer of asphalt ends. As soon as my tires hit that dropoff, they catch and make the car veer off the road. The car hits a pole and the front end of the car is bashed in. If someone asked me what happened to my car, I would likely say I hit a pole, and the pole bashed it in. But is that really the case? Or is the truth really that I failed to keep the car on the road and I bashed it in – with the pole.

The same thing is true of much, if not all, dis-ease. If I develop a pathogen-borne illness, is it the bug that caused the illness? Or did I do things through misuse or neglect to disturb my immune system so that it was not fully capable of defending against the pathogen? I read recently of a person who got a new tattoo, and against the advice of his tattoo artist went swimming in the Gulf of Mexico. The injury to his skin from the tattoo allowed a flesh-eating microbe to take hold, and he died a few days later.

What if I eat foods that are toxic to my body? Apparently rancid, or oxidized, fats are an irritant and cause inflammation. Inflammation of the inner lining of arteries causes the body to try to scab it over with fatty substance – cholesterol. Too much deposit of cholesterol causes poor blood circulation to the heart. Was the resulting heart attack caused by excess fats, or excess oxidized fats?

I read about a study that revealed that almost 8 in 10 soldiers killed in action in the Korean war had signs of coronary atherosclerosis. These are mostly young men! What they didn't take into effect is what the soldiers were eating. My guess would be that, especially in the basic training they received, they consumed a lot of dried food. Powdered milk. Powdered eggs. And hydrogenated oil like margarine. The process of manufacturing these foods oxidizes them. So, I wonder if the incidence of heart disease in these soldiers was due to what we (the government) were feeding them? As far as I know there have been no studies to look at this.

There's another factor in heart disease that any doctor will tell you about, but it doesn't show up much otherwise, and that's stress. In the last chapter we talked about how emotions can restrict the flow of chi in the body, with that restriction being capable of causing physical pain in addition to emotional pain. Wouldn't it seem to follow that restrictions in chi would cause disease-es, like heart disease; or infections that are evidence that the immune system isn't working the way it should; or cancer that is essentially runaway cells?

Books on emotional roots of diseases

There are several books that correlate diseases with their underlying emotional cause, or as I think of it: their emotional foundation.

One of them is Karol Truman's "Feelings Buried Alive Never Die," which also has a reference guide. The Reference Guide is a ring-bound mini-version of the chapter in "Feelings Buried Alive Never Die" that lists diseases and their emotional causes. It is a very good book, and generally our go-to reference for correlating diseases to emotions. This book was introduced to us by Gwendolyn Jones of angelsoflightandhealing.org, author of several books and also the person who introduced Ann to NAET.

Another good book that we use is Louise Hay's "You Can Heal Your Life." She has also published "Heal Your Body." This book has a center section that not only lists "Problem Areas" of the body affected and the "Probable Cause," it also lists a "New Thought Pattern" or affirmation to use to overcome that emotional issue.

The third book in our library on this subject is "The Body Is The Barometer Of The Soul: So Be Your Own Doctor" by Annette Noontil, published in Victoria, Australia.

Some other books I found through search are:

- Permanent Healing (Quantum mechanics of healing) by Daniel R. Condron

- Messages from the Body: Their Psychological Meaning by Michael J. Lincoln

These books don't necessarily agree with each other, and they don't necessarily cover all diseases. I believe however that all diseases originate from within, even if they seem to be caused by external factors. Remember the analogy of hitting the pole? Even though it looked like the pole did the damage, it was really my inattention.

One thing that I have found very interesting is that many, if not all, of the dis-ease to emotion correlations are very symbolic. Take for instance fear causing brain cancer. What happens when you are fearful? Your mind races, like putting your foot on the accelerator when the car is in park, and letting the engine RPMs go wild. A car engine would suffer a catastrophic failure. So does the brain, but it fails through the process of a cancerous growth – the growth of fear. Another example is a boil being symbolic of stagnation. If you think about any dis-ease or dis-comfort you are having, and think about it symbolically with the possibility that it might be emotionally based, often you can discover the underlying emotional cause of that discomfort. As you learn about the spiritual significance of different parts of your body, you'll begin having the "aha" moments where the discomfort-emotion connection makes sense.

"All Dis-ease Comes from a State of Unforgiveness"

Louise Hay quoted the "Course in Miracles" as stating "all dis-ease comes from a state of unforgiveness" and "whenever we are ill, we need to look around to see who it is that we need to forgive." It would seem that forgiveness is maybe one of the most important topics in our lives, if not the most important. Without forgiveness, quality of life suffers, health suffers… everything suffers! We've touched on energy or chi and how it affects both the body and the emotions. Hopefully you can see at this point the connection between the blockages created by unforgiveness and the effect that has on the body. This is critically important, because when you understand it, you will no longer allow unforgiveness to linger in your consciousness.

Myrtle Fillmore

Myrtle Fillmore was the co-founder of the Unity movement, along with her husband Charles. She was born in 1845 into a family with a history of tuberculosis. Her "life story" was that she would get tuberculosis and die of tuberculosis, like most of the rest of her family. She attended a lecture by metaphysician Dr. E.B. Weeks in 1886 where she learned of her innate potential for divine healing through the use of affirmative prayer. She developed her own technique of healing herself through affirmative prayer and affirmations of gratitude offered to her body. Through diligent exercise of this method she was able to cure herself of tuberculosis. Her husband Charles became intrigued with what Myrtle was doing and became involved as well. The following quote is taken from the Unity.org website:

> "The light of God revealed to us—the thought came to me first—that life was of God, that we were inseparably one with the Source, and that we inherited from the divine and perfect Father. What that revelation did to me at first was not apparent to the senses. But it held my mind above negation, and I began to claim my birthright and to act as though I believed myself the child of God, filled with His life. I gained. Others saw that there was something new in me. They asked me

> to share it. I did. Others were healed, and began to study. My husband continued his business, and at first took little interest in what I was doing. But after a time he became absorbed in the study of Truth too. We consecrated ourselves to the Lord, and kept doing daily that which we felt led to do. We began to prosper, a little at a time, and our health continued to improve." – Myrtle Fillmore

As Myrtle, and then Charles, were able to heal themselves, and continued to study and live this new understanding, they began to attract others who were seeing the difference in their lives. They started small study/prayer groups meeting in homes, but eventually grew to become the worldwide Unity movement. You can learn more about this at Unity.org. Also, there is a book available: "Myrtle Fillmore's Healing Letters" that describes her methods in more detail, in the form of letters that she had written to others.

Rather than dying of tuberculosis at a young age, Myrtle passed in 1931 of natural causes at the age of 86. Clearly the mind and thoughts have a profound influence on the health and well-being of the body.

Find additional healing at http://theenergyofforgiveness.com/chapter-8 .

Chapter 9
The Penalty For Unforgiveness

> *"Forgiveness is not always easy. At times, it feels more painful than the wound we suffered, to forgive the one that inflicted it. And yet, there is no peace without forgiveness."*
> — Marianne Williamson

Relationships

We've covered the concepts of spiritual energy "chi" and how thoughts and emotions can affect chi as well as chi influencing emotions. We've covered how this effect on chi can also affect our health. There are other factors in life that are also affected and damaged by a state of unforgiveness.

Relationships are a big factor in unforgiveness. Can you imagine a scenario where you did something that I didn't like, and through my unforgiveness I keep taunting you about it and never let you forget about it? If the we were close you might tolerate that for awhile. But at some point you would realize that enough is enough, and our relationship would start to suffer. No relationship can thrive in the presence of ill will. Eventually it will break down and die. Unforgiveness kills relationships.

When the relationship dies, the unforgiver then experiences the grieving process, which will likely lead to blaming the other, anger, and generally further reason, at least in their eyes, for being angry and unforgiving. This negative attitude further poisons the person's outlook on life. Do you see the downward trend?

Isolation

If unforgiveness kills relationships, then it will certainly also lead to isolation. Let's face it: life is full of events and circumstances that we don't like. If a person is unwilling to forgive one person or situation, there will always be something that the next person does that needs forgiveness as well. While there's an endless supply of people, eventually it gets tiresome, or the word gets out that the unforgiving person is difficult, and other people will shy away.

An underlying problem is that if I can't forgive others, then I can't forgive myself. If I can't forgive myself, then eventually I will decide that I am not worth the effort of trying to get along with other people, and just give up on relationships in general.

People tend to fall into one of two groups – those who are energized by being around other people and those who find their energy drained by other people. You might think of it as extroverts and introverts, although I'm not sure that exactly corresponds with a person being either energized or drained by others. It might seem that for the introverts, being isolated would be a good thing – that they would be more comfortable being isolated. That may be true to an extent, but despite the existence of hermits, I believe that each individual is bet-

The Energy of Forgiveness

ter off with at least the possibility of positive interaction with others. The saying goes: no man is an island. If a person becomes isolated because they can't (read that "won't") forgive, they suffer for it. They may feel comfortable in their isolation, but their life is not going to be as good as it would be in some form of community.

Law of Attraction

I've mentioned the Law of Attraction previously in this book. My condensed version of the Law of Attraction is this: "Whatever you put energy into gets bigger." You can interpret the meaning of the word "energy" in this context in two different ways, and both are valid.

One way is that you put physical "blood, sweat, and tears" energy into something. So for instance, if you want a bigger hole in the ground, you put the physical energy into digging. If you want more money, you put physical energy into whatever it is that you do to create money. If you want a relationship to be better, you do things to encourage that to happen, like telling the person you care about them, doing thoughtful and considerate deeds, and so forth. It's obvious how this works.

Another way this could be interpreted is that the "energy" is chi. "How do I do that?" you might wonder. You put chi energy into something through your thoughts, word and prayers, as well as deeds. I posted this thought to the RulesOfTheSpirit.com website recently:

Paul McKinley

> "The Law of Attraction, at least as I understand it, says that whatever you put energy into gets bigger.
>
> So I ask you: where/what are you putting energy into?
>
> Be careful what you pray for, and remember: every thought, word, or action is a prayer.
>
> I recommend disciplining yourself to put energy exclusively into things that serve your highest good - things that you will enjoy or will help you grow. Let go of the things that you don't like or that you feel upset about. Starve them of your energy."

There are two levels to this concept of being careful of your thoughts. One level is that *it messes with your mind.* If your thoughts are focused on a certain thing, and that's what you're thinking about a lot, those thoughts tend to drown out everything else. It's helpful to understand the world as an ever-moving and infinite soup of possibilities, objects, and events. If your thoughts are focused on one thing, then that's what you're going to notice. Things or events that don't correspond with what you're thinking about become, as "Hitchhiker's Guide to the Galaxy" author Douglas Adams put it, "Somebody Else's Problem" and thus it is invisible to you. If you are infatuated with the concept of a red corvette, and all you think about is a red corvette, you're not going to even see the silver one, or even the red Lotus or any other car on the road for that matter. The bottom line is you're going to suddenly start noticing the whatever-it-is – in this case red corvettes - that were *already* floating around in that soup of possibility you live in.

The Energy of Forgiveness

The other level is that the Law of Attraction works through a spiritual process as well. Through Spirit action, *things* are created from *no-thing*. Well, it's not actually created out of no-thing; it's created from the infinite supply of Spirit energy, which in the physical universe appears to be no-thing. Einstein was made famous by his equation $E=mc^2$. Do you really understand what that means? It means that mass is compressed energy – compressed by a factor that corresponds to the square of the speed of light (which is energy). *And*, Spirit energy doesn't just create matter! Remember that space and time has no meaning in spirit. Spirit energy also creates circumstances – events, synchronicities. Because space and time has no meaning in spirit, it's just as easy – or maybe easier – to create something ten years ago so that something else will happen now.

Okay, so what does that have to do with forgiveness, or in this context, unforgiveness?

We've already discussed how unforgiveness is a negative emotion. It really doesn't feel good. It restricts the life energy chi. Through the action of chi restriction, it results in dis-comfort and dis-ease in the body. It destroys relationships. So the more you put energy into unforgiveness, the more that energy, through the Law of Attraction, creates events that are going to be unpleasant for you – events that are going to need, on your part: forgiveness. As I am unforgiving about one thing, that unforgiveness creates another. Now I am unforgiving about two things. Those two things each create another. Now I have four. As the energy builds around unforgiveness, the return gets greater. Two events may create five instead of four, or four may create twelve. Life gets pretty miserable when my energy attracts things that need forgiveness.

Self-destruction and Disease

Self destruction and disease go together. We've already discussed disease, so let's move on to self-destruction. I have mentioned that if I am unforgiving of others, I will also be unforgiving of myself. Actually it's more likely that I will be unforgiving of myself, because the hardest one to forgive is the self. I previously mentioned the quote "Refusing to forgive is like taking a poison and expecting the other person to get sick." Interestingly, unforgiveness of self is exactly the only way that this analogy works. I modified that quote to make it a bit more like the real thing – it's on the inside leaf of this book. It is:

"Refusing to forgive is like grabbing a red hot poker and shaking it at the unforgiven."

Now imagine picking up a red-hot poker and shaking it at someone because you're upset with them. As soon as you pick it up, you will start feeling a vibration that is the water in your skin boiling. If you took your hand away immediately, you would see that your skin has become scorched and white. If you hold the poker long enough, it might actually catch your skin on fire. Did you know that your skin and flesh will actually burn? Certainly in very short order the skin will be damaged enough that it would have to be regrown. A little longer and the muscles and tendons would have to be regrown. Much longer, and the hand would have to be regrown, except that I'm not aware of anyone actually regrowing

The Energy of Forgiveness

a hand. This is a rather graphic example, but it illustrates the destructive power of unforgiveness – and the one that unforgiveness damages is the one that needs to do the forgiving.

Another aspect is that if I am unforgiving, and hence unforgiving of myself, I am likely to engage in self-destructive behavior. It might be just banging myself on the head, or being careless with what I am doing because there's no real reason to care for myself. It could even go into more drastic behaviors like anorexia, depression, or suicide.

Holding another down takes your own energy

Imagine that you are engaged in a wrestling match. Your objective is to hold the other person down. The thing is, it takes all your strength to do that. The longer you struggle to hold them down, the more you become fatigued. And, most importantly, as long as you're holding the other person down, you can't get up and walk away. The two of you are kind of stuck together there, for better or for worse, until one of you decides to give up and walk away.

Unforgiveness can be a bit like that. It takes energy to maintain a negative attitude towards someone. Even if you feel like you're justified in being upset with them, it still takes your energy, not theirs, to maintain that ill will. Holding on to the unforgiveness over time will cause fatigue. You will likely experience this as a feeling of tiredness or being irritable.

Paul McKinley

Pay me now or pay me later

One thing I've observed over time is that the emotions of an event, especially a difficult one, need to be experienced. If I experience the death of a pet, I have a need to experience the emotions that go along with that. I need to go through the grieving process. If I don't process them, they will fester and continue to poison my life experience until I do process them. One of the books I mentioned earlier is titled "Feelings Buried Alive Never Die" – and this is what the title of the book is referring to.

This topic was revisited many times in the popular television series Star Trek, in the character of Mr. Spock. Mr. Spock came from a race of people who had decided that they must purge all emotions, lest they destroy themselves. They had essentially bred emotions out of themselves. Their entire culture was based on the elimination of emotion from consciousness. Do you know of families or people who have adopted a "no emotion" attitude? But Mr. Spock was presented as half-human. As a half-human, Mr. Spock still experienced emotions, but through his upbringing and the society where he was raised, he was not able to properly express or experience those emotions. As a result, all sorts of situations arose where he discovered the value of being able to process the emotions in a healthy way.

The challenge with this is that the emotions don't go away. You may even feel that you've managed to put things away, but the reality is that they continue to fester, if not in your conscious mind, then in the subconscious mind. And, in my experience, they don't just sit there – they fester. The boil grows until eventually it erupts. The best time to process emotions is as soon after the event as possible. Yes, sometimes it's better to delay the processing a bit. If a bull is chasing you across the pasture, it's better to delay processing the disappointment of having had to abandon your picnic lunch and basket in the middle of the pasture. But still, the sooner, the better. It's pay me now, or pay me later, and if it's later it will be plus interest.

Family standards can get a bit interesting here. In my family, positive emotions were okay, but negative emotions were not. So negative emotions had to be suppressed. Anger, fear, grieving and so forth had to be experienced privately where nobody could see and disapprove. Ann's family, on the other hand, rejected all emotions both positive and negative. So there wasn't even the opportunity for the positive emotions to balance out the negative ones. And that, in my opinion, is what resulted in her panic attacks.

This has a lot to do with forgiveness. Forgiving is the process of resolving the negative emotions related to an event. If I can get myself to a place of having experienced and worked through the disappointment or other negative emotions related to an event quickly and easily, it makes it easier to move on with life and continue to grow. If I hold on to the unforgiveness, the interest accrues, and the difficulty of clearing that issue from my life becomes more and more difficult and costly.

"What dreams may come"

There was a movie titled "What Dreams May Come" starring Robin Williams and Annabella Sciorra that illustrates beautifully, if somewhat tearfully for the viewer, the effects of lack of forgiveness. It starts out as a love story between the two characters Chris and Annie, but then their two children are killed in a car crash, and then later Chris is killed in a car crash. Chris finds himself in "heaven" but then learns that Annie has committed suicide and is in "hell." Chris goes to rescue her, with the help of a friend and their son. The friend keeps telling Chris that it can't be done, that because Annie has committed suicide she won't be able to let go of her own self-unforgiveness. But Chris goes anyway, and decides that if he can't rescue her, he will just stay with her in her hell. His willingness to sacrifice himself makes the difference for her. She realizes that she can't allow him to join her in hell, and they both escape hell's grip.

Some of the things that are portrayed in the movie really underscore the role of forgiveness in life. At one point in order to get to Annie, Chris had to walk across a landscape that was people's faces imbedded in the ground. The faces were all of people who were suffering from the fruits of their own unforgiveness – either anger at others, or unforgiveness of themselves. When he finally gets to Annie, she is absorbed with all the things that are wrong. She doesn't recognize Chris or even that she is dead, and she still blames herself for both her children's and her husband's deaths. It is only through Chris's forgiveness of her, and forgiveness of himself that he is able to bring her back.

I believe that if there is such a thing as hell, it is as the movie depicted in the sense that each of the denizens of hell have created their own image of hell, and have the choice in each moment of whether to stay or whether to leave. It is their own clinging to the hurtful experiences they had in life that keeps them there. It is their unwillingness to forgive that keeps them in misery. Being in hell is not a punishment from God, but rather the individual punishing themself.

Blocking Abundance

How would you feel if you gave me a dollar and I immediately tore it up, burned it, or threw it in the toilet? Would you keep giving me dollar after dollar to see if I was going to do something else with it, even though I kept destroying them? How do you think it would work if every dollar you received you cursed it and threw it away, would you be able to accumulate enough to do the things you needed or wanted to do, considering that in this world most things work through the action of money? That's a little like what it is to be unforgiving. Energy workers understand that abundance comes through the flow of chi. Anything that restricts or disturbs the flow of chi also limits the ability to experience abundance, at least an abundance of things we enjoy.

Conversely, how would you feel if you gave me a dollar, and my face lit up with joy and I thanked you and gave you a hug. When you gave me another dollar, I thanked you and talked about how I was going to use that dollar to create something wonderful. When you gave me another dollar, I lit up once again and dreamed aloud of how I could use that dollar to help the neighbor who was in need. Is that a different feeling than when I destroyed each dollar? It's my understanding that gratitude is also a key to experiencing abundance.

Paul McKinley

It's not that Spirit needs to feel good about creating abundance, not at all. Spirit creates for me whatever I ask – whatever I put energy into - whether it's something I like or something I don't like. No, it's that when I maintain an attitude of gratitude, when I really feel joy about the abundance that manifests itself in my life; when I experience the positive emotions surrounding the things that are created for me and given to me, I am aligning myself with that experience. The more energy I put into it, the bigger it gets.

Imagine two tuning forks tuned to the same pitch. If I strike one fork so that it "sings" and place it near the second tuning fork, the second tuning fork will begin to vibrate also. This could be because of the sound waves from the first fork striking the second. It could also be due to the molecular electro-magnetic-gravitational waves communicating between the two forks. If the second fork is not tuned fairly close to the first, it will vibrate some, but not nearly as well as if they are tuned together. I will hardly be able to tell that it's vibrating.

Unforgiveness works the same. By resonating with things I don't like, things I don't want, things I consider "ugly," I begin to activate in that "soup of possibility" exactly that: things I don't want and won't enjoy. If I want abundance in my life, the restrictions in my chi that are the result of restricting the flow by hanging on to the unforgiveness will also resonate with restricting abundance. That's not to say I can't experience abundance if I am unforgiving, but rather that it won't be as much, nor will it be as easy.

The Energy of Forgiveness

Want more? See http://theenergyofforgiveness.com/chapter-9.

Chapter 10
When Forgiving Seems Impossible

*"Holding on is believing that there's a past;
letting go is knowing that there's a future."*
— Daphne Rose Kingma

Relief at last!

By now you may be reeling from all of the "bad" stuff we've discussed regarding unforgiveness. Unforgiveness is hard on your mind. Unforgiveness is hard on your body. Unforgiveness is hard on your spirit. Unforgiveness is hard on your life.

But we've covered all that negative aspects now. Hopefully by now you've begun to understand what forgiveness is, how important it is, and maybe most importantly that unforgiveness is not a viable option. You know by now that you must learn to forgive quickly and easily, for your own best interest. Unforgiveness doesn't help anyone, and the one it hurts most is the unforgiving one.

The challenge may be that you have a habit of being unforgiving. Your "forgive" muscles are weak and unused. You still struggle with forgiving, especially in the situations where you now recognize you need the most to forgive.

The journey, at least for this book, is almost over. This is the last chapter. But it's also the chapter where I offer some solace in the form of techniques to help you get those forgiveness muscles some exercise and fitness. Along with the information you've learned so far in this book, *this* chapter covers the tools you need to forgive *quickly* and *easily*.

But the journey isn't over for you, it's just beginning. It is a glorious journey! Imagine you have been climbing a mountain. You've struggled with the slope, and the brush, and the unstable gravelly ground. You've slipped backwards a few times and skinned your knees. But you're almost to the top now. You're beginning to get glimpses of the beautiful vista on the other side, the pot of gold at the end of the rainbow. The rest of the journey will take some time, and there will be a few more times where you earn some more abrasions and bruises. But armed with your new knowledge, you'll have the tools you need to live a fuller, more abundant life, without the baggage of unforgiveness.

Hold on, here we go!

The behavioral learning process

There's a process for learning new behaviors and habits. I mentioned this in *The Rules of the Spirit*, but we'll review it again here because it's important to understand this process. I want you to feel *good* about how you are progressing, and avoid heaping unforgiveness on yourself for taking time to integrate the habit of forgiving quickly and easily. It's a process, and it will be easier for some people than for others.

The Energy of Forgiveness

The first stage of this process is that you don't recognize that anything is amiss. I'm going to use the example of "I keep stepping on your toes" as an innocuous example. You can substitute whatever behavior *you* have or someone else has that you find is causing an issue. The transgression, nor the degree of transgression does not matter, it's the *process* that I'm explaining here.

So, I step on your toes. I don't notice that I'm stepping on your toes, so I don't recognize this as an issue. But *you* of course notice I'm stepping on your toes because it's painful – to you. The first time or two you might just pass it off because you don't want to be unpleasant and you might chalk it up to just an "oops" event. But at some point you comment that I'm stepping on your toes. "Ouch!" you say. I don't have any idea why you're "Ouch!"-ing. You might tell me I'm stepping on your toes, and I might deny it at first – "Me? How could I be stepping on your toes?" It's not that I'm not taking responsibility, it's just that it's news to me and I don't see how I could be doing it. Depending on the emotional baggage between us, it may even get a bit testy. Let's expect that any emotional baggage will be abandoned at the platform as we both evolve into forgiveness.

I may go through a stage of denial, maintaining that the behavior isn't harmful or it's justified. "I wouldn't be doing it if your feet weren't sticking out there!" or "I didn't step *hard!*" or "how could *that* have hurt you?" If that is the case, at some point I also have to come to recognize the harm of the behavior.

Paul McKinley

The next stage is when I begin to recognize when I've done it... but only *after* the fact. It's hard to change behavior when I don't see that I'm doing it until it's too late – until I see your toe is turning black and blue. But it does help that at least I recognize that I'm doing it. It's undeniable at this point. I cannot change behavior that I don't recognize in myself so this is a big step. I see the behavior exists, and I understand the connection to an outcome that I didn't want or enjoy – that of you being upset with me for causing you pain or especially seeing that I've bruised you, but I feel helpless to change it. This stage lasts for... a while.

At some point I move into the next stage where I actually start seeing myself doing it *when it's happening*. I feel your foot under mine as I'm stepping on your toes. I can say from my own experience this is a very "Twilight Zone" feeling. It's where I really come to terms with the existence of what some call the "watcher" or "observer" – that part of me that stands to the side and comments on what's going on. Sometimes the "watcher" is characterized by an "angel" that sits on the shoulder. It's a bit like watching a movie where the character played is myself. Like a very predictable movie, I know what's going to happen, it's almost like a deja-vu moment. I may be internally screaming at myself like I scream at the characters in the move *"don't do it!!"* but it still plays out exactly like I know it has a thousand times before.

After another while, as I think about what happened and the unwanted consequences I now know are associated with the habit, I begin to get creative and think "what if I did *this* instead of *that*?" Even then when the situation presents itself, I still do the old thing – and get the old results. I continue the habitual behavior, even though I have what might be a better solution, and I actually see myself doing it as it happens. This is the stage that fits what the Apostle Paul was describing when he wrote "that which I know I should do, I do not, and that which I know I should not do, that is what I do." (Romans 7:15) But as I see myself doing the "wrong" thing, I also start seeing myself doing something better. This is progress! It may not be very satisfying, but it's progress!

Eventually I start catching myself in the act, and early enough to actually choose to do one of those scenarios I've been rehearsing in my imagination. It may be that my new twist works out better, it may not. But the point is I intentionally did *something different!* I'd bet the chances are that the new behavior turned out better. After all, even though the behavior is new and therefore experimental, it's based on *thought* rather than *habit*. I'll place my bets on a response that is consciously thought out rather than a knee-jerk any day.

One day, I start responding to the same event in such a way that the result is much better, much more in line with what I want. It may be that in the process I've come to understand at a more basic level what is going on underneath the event and have not just one good response, but a recipe for any number of good responses based on an understanding of the mechanics of the circumstance.

How does that relate to forgiving? It's all about my response to "*the event.*" If my response to an event I don't like is to explode into an irrational rage, it may take me awhile to go through this process and learn to recognize that a level-headed response to any given event is probably going to yield better results. It may be that I need to learn to reframe what's going on rather than racing to the blame game. I discuss reframing in the next section. There are infinite possibilities of "events" that can produce a need to forgive, and each type of event may require that I use this process to move quickly and easily to the end-game of forgiving quickly and easily.

Reframing

I learned this method from Ann. Let's say I'm driving down the road, and someone zips by and cuts in front of me, almost clipping my car. I could get really upset with them and do any number of possibly dangerous retaliations. Fortunately, I've mostly outgrown those responses and now my usual reaction is to just grumble "some people really should not be driving." Then I laugh about it and let it go. Ann's response is to wonder what's going on in that person's life that they would do such a dangerous thing and put the people around them at risk. She runs through various imaginary scenarios in her head: maybe they have a relative who is having an emergency, or they just had an argument with someone and are upset. You can see there's any number of different scenarios that could produce less-than-pleasant behavior.

Ann's attitude, other than her just plain being more compassionate than I am, came from an experience in her high school years. She was always upset when a neighbor drove too fast through the neighborhood, because she was concerned for her cats' safety. She had several that were killed by being hit by cars. She was outside one Sunday afternoon, and one of her neighbors

The Energy of Forgiveness

went tearing through the neighborhood. She yelled angrily at the car as it raced by. The next day at school, she learned that one of her fellow high-school students who lived down the street, a piccolo player in the band, had been in a bad car accident in Houston. Her parents were notified, and told if they wanted to see their daughter alive, they better hurry to the hospital because she wasn't going to be alive much longer. She never really knew whether that was actually the girl's parents racing down the road and they were the ones she was yelling at angrily. After that she came to realize that she *didn't know* what other people are experiencing – what is going on in their life – that makes them behave in a way that she didn't agree with. It lends new meaning to "walk a mile in their shoes." Their shoes usually don't fit you so there's no way to really understand what they are experiencing.

Now, you might have heard situations where this reframing or "rationalization" response could be part of a codependency relationship, such as an abused spouse making excuses for their abusive partner. But in an abusive relationship, the abused partner is making excuses for repeated violations and setting themselves up for more abuse. This is not the same thing.

What I want you to understand is that in many or most situations, you really don't know what's going on with the other person. Recognize that anything you might think about a situation is just a story you made up for yourself, to explain the behavior. Any story you might imagine about why they are behaving the way they do is just that – a story. Ann's attitude is, if you're going to totally make up a story about someone, why not make up a story that is compassionate? Why not make up one that allows you to feel positive about the situation rather than negative? Would you rather be thinking "wow, that person is a dangerous idiot!" or "Oh, I pray that whatever is bothering them gets resolved quickly and happily!"

Do you see the difference in your own energy? Do you feel the difference you create *in yourself* by how you respond to difficult events? You can choose how you respond to any given event. Your choice can keep your vibration high, or you can choose a response that lowers your vibration. I recommend choosing the response that always brings your vibration higher because, by that means, you will constantly be improving your life.

EFT – again!

I mentioned EFT earlier in this book. EFT is such a wonderful way to eliminate any negative emotions, as well as any pain or other baggage that goes with it. I'll give you an example from my own experience.

I had an encounter with someone in a leadership position who spent two hours lecturing me on something that was precipitated by someone else who was engaging in triangulation. I had shown a video in a group situation – it happened to be the second bar room scene from "A Beautiful Mind" – to illustrate the point that the "every man for himself" attitude doesn't work, but rather the potential outcome for every member of the group is better when the group members work together. Unfortunately, this scene is couched in rather sexist terms, and the "triangulator" was offended. Rather than addressing it with me they went to the leadership per-

The Energy of Forgiveness

son. As a result, I got to "enjoy" two hours of irrational rant, where I was not given any opportunity to explain or defend myself. The underlying story is that the leader was coming from a place of fear, so their behavior wasn't as rational as it could have been. I couldn't even speak – the person couldn't "hear" me through their fear. So all I could do is wait for them to wind down. At any rate, I left that meeting absolutely furious. I was ready to walk away from the organization even though it was an important part of my life. I felt I had been wronged on many levels. Anger is always built on a foundation of fear, so part of what *I* was feeling was *fear* – fear that all I had invested in this organization was about to be lost.

Because I was experiencing so much anger over this situation, and because I don't want to have that kind of energy in my life, and finally because I realize that I am probably not going to make good decisions while I am experiencing that kind and level of anger, I asked Ann to work with me on this issue using EFT, so that I could let it go. We spent about 15 minutes on it in one session. I remember I had the weirdest feeling afterwards. Imagine a balloon somewhere in your psyche. You can't really put a finger on it, but it's there and you can feel it. This balloon is so full that it's about to burst. There's a palpable tension, and what's inside that balloon isn't pleasant. When we were done, I could "feel" where that balloon *had been*. But it wasn't there anymore. It was like there was a void where that balloon. filled with unmentionable, had been before. But it was gone. It was palpably gone. The tension was gone. The balloon was empty, in fact it didn't even exist anymore. It didn't pop, it just faded to nothing. There was no longer any anger, or fear, associated with the event. None.

As a result, I was able to easily let the situation go; to "fail" to react to it if you will. Clearly I remember the situation and how I felt at the time – I did tell the story here. I didn't care much for the leader as it's hard for me to follow someone who leads out of fear. I understand it but I don't respect it. And frankly the leader wasn't around for long after that. I remained friends with the triangulator. I didn't care much for that person either, because I knew how they would behave under certain circumstances. As well, we were just on different wavelengths both intellectually and spiritually so it was hard for us to relate to one another. We both spoke English, and yet we spoke different languages. But we were still friends. We could interact and do what each of us needed to do for sake of the organization without any animosity.

Through EFT, I was able to remember the event, but be totally neutral emotionally about it. I was able to set healthy boundaries by avoiding situations that the other person would find offensive. There was and is no emotional poison in my psyche related to the event. It happened. I learned from it. It is in the past. I have moved on.

Wouldn't you like to deal with issues that are eating you from the inside out, in the course of a painless exercise that lasts a few minutes, and has permanent results, at least for that issue? That's EFT.

The Energy of Forgiveness

Play It Again, Sam: Rinse And Repeat

Finally recognize that, if you are currently having trouble forgiving quickly and easily, it is because you have not developed strength and stamina in your "forgive" muscles… yet. It will come, I assure you. I used the following quote as the introduction to the last chapter in *The Rules of the Spirit*, and it applies here as well:

> "You will rise, and you will fall, you will get discouraged, you will become encouraged. But always, you will be progressing, always. And so, you must simply stick to it, and the day will come when you will no longer say 'I hope, I desire, I pray,' but you will say 'I know.'"
>
> — Ernest Holmes

Ernest was speaking from a perspective of learning to heal yourself, and that applies in this context as well. You are learning to heal yourself. So, you must simply stick to it. Think about the things you've learned from this book. You now understand, at least intellectually, why and how forgiving is so important. You've got the stuff you need! Your task now is to put it into practice. Give yourself some time to work on it. Forgive yourself. Practice the things I've covered in this book. Re-read this book or even just the parts that seem relevant from time to time if you find yourself not remembering some of the information. It's a lot to take in at one whack. And when you find that you've fallen, pick yourself up, dust yourself off, and keep going. As the shampoo bottle says: rinse and repeat!

Paul McKinley

As a parting gift, I have a two stories that you may find amusing as well as instructive on the topic of forgiveness.

> Two traveling monks reached a river where they met a young woman. Wary of the current, she asked if they could carry her across. One of the monks hesitated, but the other quickly picked her up onto his shoulders, transported her across the water, and put her down on the other bank. She thanked him and departed.
>
> As the monks continued on their way, the one was brooding and preoccupied. Finally, unable to hold his silence, he spoke out.
>
> "Brother, our spiritual training teaches us to avoid any contact with women, but you picked that woman at the river up on your shoulders and carried her!"
>
> "Brother," the second monk replied, "I set her down on the other side and let her go. You are still carrying her."

The second story helps to remember my analogy of "Refusing to forgive is like picking up a red hot iron rod and shaking it the other person."

> One day a blacksmith was making horseshoes. As he finished a horseshoe, he would throw it red-hot out into the dirt in front of the shop to slowly cool.

The Energy of Forgiveness

The town derelict meandered over to the shop to see what the blacksmith was doing. Not understanding the process, he reached down to pick up the horseshoe the blacksmith had just thrown down, thinking to hand it back to him. When he picked up the horseshoe, he instantly felt that it was hot, so instead of gently picking it up he flung it violently overhead.

The blacksmith commented drily "A bit warm, wasn't it?"

The derelict replied: "No, it just doesn't take me long to look at a horseshoe."

May you always dispatch your forgiveness as quickly!

Continue the learning! http://theenergyofforgiveness.com/chapter-10

ABOUT THE AUTHOR

International spiritual teacher and author Paul McKinley was born in Virginia, grew up mostly in San Antonio Texas and educated at the University of Texas, where he earned a Bachelor degree in Mechanical Engineering. Mr. McKinley has had a widely-varied career starting as a water-well pipe-stabber, motorcycle mechanic, research assistant, and engineer. As an engineer he worked on projects ranging from designing computer equipment to robotic aircraft part manufacturing to automated bowling ball manufacturing. He moved to providing computer support and eventually worked 15 years as an independent consultant providing expertise on High Availability Clustering.

When he was twenty-two his brother Mike was killed in a helicopter crash, which started him on a lifelong journey of spiritual discovery and enlightenment. For a time he served as a Methodist Layspeaker, before being introduced to the Unity movement at a screening of the movie "The People Vs. The State of Illusion" by Austin Vickers at Unity Church of the Hills in Austin Texas. He served as a rotational speaker for Unity of Temple and also spoke on The Law of Attraction at the Unitarian church in Temple Texas before moving back to Virginia with his wife Ann, also a born Virginian.

Paul currently lives in Virginia with his wife Ann and three cats. He teaches spiritual concepts, especially forgiveness, internationally as well as running a local computer business. He is also an energy healer, practicing Reiki and a similar method that he developed prior to his Reiki attunement.

Printed in Poland
by Amazon Fulfillment
Poland Sp. z o.o., Wrocław